The Listening Project

Stories and Resources for Transformative Personal and Community Change

by Herb Walters with Geoff Huggins

ISBN 978-1-365-33451-1

Published by The Listening Project, 965 White Oak Rd. Burnsville, NC 28714

Further information about The Listening Project: www.listeningproject.org or HerbRSVP@gmail.com

Table of Contents

Inspiration from Unknown Heroines and Heroes

Thanks and love to these special people and organizations that have inspired and helped, including:

It has been three decades since the first Listening Project. Looking back, I can remember so many people I have worked with—people whom I believe to be some of the great, unheralded heroes and heroines of our time. They give deeply from their lives for the betterment of others. In the midst of their busy lives, they give with dedication and wisdom and with less reward than they deserve. They do this not because they think they are natural leaders, but because they are willing to do what it takes, make mistakes, learn and grow, and to find joy in service.

Thanks and love to:

- Usha Ruark, Geoff Huggins, Marie Marcella, Dixie Pomerat, Annalisa Littleton, Florence Yaffe, Jim Lenhart, and other editorial helpers
- All past and present Listening Project/RSVP staff including Marnie, Catherine Peck, Judy Scheckel, Jenifer Morgan, Jim Lenhart, Merelyn McKnight, Tom Fischer, David Grant, Claire Hanrahan, Joseph Heflin, Bill Hartsock, Ward McCallister, Aaron Thompson, Sam Ruark, Dixie Pomerat, Barry Williams
- Past and current Listening Project/RSVP board members, volunteers and all who have conducted Listening Projects
- All the donors and foundations that made our work possible, with special thanks to Julian Price, Frances Moore Lappé', Eunice Wagner, Phillip Blumenthal, Ted and Trudy Winsberg, Meg McLeod; David, Judith, &Ty; Lela Love
- Arthur Morgan School (special thanks to the late Ernest Morgan)
- Thich Nhat Hanh and Carl Rogers
- Celo Friends (Quaker) Meeting and Celo Community Land Trust Inc.
- Jim Allen and the Vine and Fig Tree Community
- U.S. and International Fellowship of Reconciliation
- American Friends Service Committee

Introduction & Helpful Information from the Author

In 1981, I founded Rural Southern Voice for Peace (RSVP). It was a publication that focused on social change in rural communities in the southeast U.S. – a region notorious for resisting change. In 1986, I developed the first Listening Project for a grassroots organization that was not connecting well with their community. They were in fact pretty isolated. The results of this first Community Listening Project were really exciting – it opened doors and expanded outreach and effectiveness. So I put the word out about the Listening Project and the rest is history. In this book you have accounts of local, national and international Listening Projects that have helped organizations achieve transformational grassroots organizing and action. The stories herein are from the late 80's to the present. Whether old or new, each story can inspire and inform current and future efforts to create a better world.

FYI: I do not remember exactly when it happened but our organization, Rural Southern Voice for Peace (*RSVP)* was at some point, renamed *Listening Project*. This change reflected our total focus on providing training and resources for Community Listening Projects and Facilitated Group Listening (FGL) programs.

Protecting the Privacy of Listening Project Participants

In some cases the identities of people and their communities have been left out or changed. Listening Project interviews are offered as safe spaces with commitments of confidentiality. In cases where permission has been granted, we use people's names.

PART I

Transformative Change That Starts with Listening

> *People are hungry to be truly listened to! In many cases, when a dialogue with good listening is finally over, something very important has happened. It is the formation of a positive human relationship between two people who had previously been on different sides of the fence.*

Chapter 1

Hungry for Listening, Hungry for Change

Divisiveness, Alienation, Fear, Disempowerment...

These are some of the causes and responses to our troubled world.

Corporations, politicians, and all the power brokers and material goods we often look to for our well-being, cannot bring the changes we seek. But we, the people, can - one step at a time. It begins with changing ourselves and depends on our ability to develop resources that enable us to skillfully and creatively work with others – including those people whom we might now see as our opposition.

Listening Projects are a resource that for 30+ years has helped transform possibility into reality. What is a Listening Project made of? It takes skillful organizing and action that are rooted in listening, empathy and determination. This includes:

- Reflection and exploration of new ideas and possibilities

- Skillful and creative organizational development

- Grassroots empowerment and creative, community-based solutions

These skills can also transform our personal lives and relationships. This book provides guidance and coaching on how to skillfully apply deep listening in all areas of our lives. Most information, however, is provided in the form of inspiring stories from individuals and communities that have experienced the transformative power of deep listening and community action.

These stories can open your heart and spark your own creative imagination, compassion, and determination.

TAKING ACTION

When compassion urges us to take action to help, how do we respond? What can I do? That is the tough question that often stumps us. Whether it be a disagreement with a friend or neighbor, a neighborhood crisis, or pervasive problems—such as personal, local, and international conflict, injustice or environmental degradation—it is easy to feel powerless or confused about what to do.

Another difficulty is that if we respond too impulsively to the call to do something to help, our action may be inspired by anger or self-righteousness. Although our first impulse may have been to help, we can end up alienating or coercing people, creating further barriers to positive change.

It is helpful to have some tools that can support us in our desire to help. One of the most effective tools we have at our disposal is the simple act of listening. Simple, yes, but listening is also an art. With care and experience, it can become "deep listening" which can transform our own lives and those whom we listen to. Several inspiring personal stories throughout this book will help you see the possibilities that await you as you develop your own listening skills.

Deep Listening, also known as active listening, is at the heart of the Listening Project, developed in 1986 by Herb Walters, and Rural Southern Voice for Peace (RSVP), founded in 1981. Listening Projects combine several potent elements that can lead to transformative change at both the personal and the community level.

DEEP LISTENING …

There is a difference between hearing what someone says and truly listening. In a Listening Project, we have a genuine interest in understanding the other person. We are asking questions and listening, not just to the other person's words, but also to their underlying feelings, needs, concerns, hopes, and beliefs. We are open to the totality of the other person.

This kind of listening takes us to a deeper understanding of, or empathy for, the person to whom we are listening. Our empathy can then help us feel compassion—even for a person with whom we have serious disagreements. This can have a dramatic effect on your relationship. Rather than reacting to your negative judgments, the other person can usually sense that you care. Therefore, she or he is more likely to feel safe enough to do some self-reflection and consider new ideas and possibilities.

This process of opening to change is not a one-way street. It is equally important that our listening enables us to become more open-minded and considerate. It helps us feel safe to explore our current thinking as well as new ideas and solutions.

Deep listening can also help uncover common ground that would probably never have been found if you had simply tried to convince or change the other person. You know what it is like when someone comes to your door wants to convert you to their beliefs. We tend to feel defensive of our own beliefs. We do not really want to spend our time with someone like that.

In deep listening interviews, even those that engage two opposing sides, people don't want the listener to stop spending time with them. People are hungry to be truly listened to. Deep listening doesn't happen frequently in us in society, but when it does, individuals can rise above their fears and explore common values and concerns.

Personal Change & Development of Positive Relationships ...

Deep listening can reveal new possibilities for personal healing and change for both the listener and those we listen to. It can also be a spiritual process that helps us step outside our usual ways of reacting to others. The Religious Society of Friends, or Quakers, calls this "seeking the spirit of God in both friend and foe."

Deep listening develops our own capacity for empathy, compassion, and creativity, which can improve our relationships with family, friends, foes, and strangers. It can be applied in your

8

personal life and, if you so choose, in the work of social change. When a dialogue with a good listener is finally over, it often results in the formation of a positive human relationship between people who may or may not have agreed at the beginning.

Community Organizing

Community organizing can be defined as people in an organization, neighborhood, town, county, or other form of community working together within an organizational structure that empowers them to achieve mutually agreed-upon goals. It empowers individuals and impacted communities whose voices might otherwise be overlooked or ignored.

It begins when one or more organizations work together to develop the resources needed to conduct their Listening Project. This includes training teams of listeners to conduct and record deep listening interviews with numerous individuals in the community. It continues throughout the project and is especially important after most or all listening interviews are processed and understood. What is learned from these interviews provides a foundation for collaborative community action that can result in grassroots community-based change.

Collaborative Community Action …

Listening Projects enable greater numbers of individuals, groups, and organizations to collaborate (work together) to bring about positive change that is rooted in the voices and the priorities of the people. This then can result in positive and even transformative, community-based change. Below are some of the stories that will inform and inspire you.

Other Uses of Deep Listening

Keep in mind that there are many ways to connect listening with personal concerns or social change— even if it is just taking time to listen and discuss controversial issues with people who have different ideas from yours.

Most people who do good work in their communities are not natural born activists. They are everyday people who decided to contribute in some small or big way to create change in their neighborhood, community organization, church, city, county, state, or nation.

Here is an exercise you can do to help you clarify how listening has already benefited your personal, social, and work relationships.

Remember a time when listening really made a difference in your life—either when someone listened to you during a time of need, or when you listened to someone who benefited. Reflect on some of the feelings you had during this experience. Then answer these two questions:

1. How did listening affect you?

2. How did listening affect the other person?

Chapter 2

Herb's Journey to Listening

I grew up in a working class, military family that was stationed overseas in Texas and Georgia, where we ultimately settled. The Vietnam War and the Civil Rights movement were formative political events in my life.

Despite my conservative, military family upbringing, I became a conscientious objector to the war in Vietnam. I could not, in good conscience kill others no matter what the reason. I engaged in anti-war organizing and protest, and during that time I became aware that some of the actions of the anti-war movement were alienating a large section of the Americans. Our nation was polarized and there was very little listening or dialogue.

As was the case in many homes, my family was torn apart by the war. My father, a sergeant in the U.S. Army, could agree with my feelings about racial equality but he could not understand or tolerate my opposition to U.S. intervention in Vietnam. I wanted so much for my parents to understand what I was feeling, but any attempt at discussion resulted in all of us being frustrated and upset, to say the least. My father's fierce anger and his sporadic use of physical force were painful both emotionally and physically.

Then one day, I realized that if I wanted my Dad to understand and respect me, I needed to deepen my understanding of him. So I decided to walk a mile in his shoes.

Herbert Valentine Walters, my Dad, grew up on a farm. He was a hard-working, honorable career soldier who joined the Army during WWII to protect his family and his country from the fascists trying to rule the world. My Dad went on to fight in Korea and Vietnam, feeling that was his contribution to creating peace. Simply put, he saw war as a necessary means to keep us from being killed or dominated by others, and he believed in peace and the dream of America. Our over-arching values were quite similar—the details not so— and I began to see that there was room for mutual understanding and respect. I gave him mine even though he wasn't able to do the same for me until he was on his deathbed.

When my Dad was found to have cancer, doctors suspected it was induced by Agent Orange, the chemical used in Vietnam to kill vegetation so our bombs could find their human targets. One of my strongest final memories of my Dad as he was dying was seeing him look out the hospital window at the flowers, grass, and trees. He had spent so many hours nurturing his food and flower gardens. As a retired and disabled vet, he could spend hours just digging and growing in a yard that was a thousand times smaller than the farm he grew up on.

In his final days, Dad was on oxygen and I had to help him over to the window where he could look outside his hospital room. As he looked out over the park below, he released a long and peaceful sigh and shook his head. I think he was reflecting on the immense beauty of life captured in the simplicity of flowers and trees. He surely knew he would be leaving that, and so much more behind, with his imminent passing. He turned to me and said, "Son, you were right. There's just too much killing these days."

A short time later as he lay in his hospital bed, unable to get up again, I lay my head on him and I told him much I loved and respected him. An hour later he released his last breath.

Throughout this experience, I kept wishing that there was some way for people on different sides of difficult issues to hear and understand one another. With race riots in the streets of the city we lived in, and a nightly Vietnam kill count on the TV news each night, I had yet to find answers to that question. But a small but important event soon occurred that opened a few windows.

A journalism teacher I had in second year of college told everyone to write a paper on the war in Vietnam. That was great, I thought. I had plenty to say.

Then, however, he added that our assignment was to support the position that was the opposite of our own. That idea startled me. I

12

didn't really like it, but it was an assignment and I did it. When I finished I felt something had changed in me.

I had slowly but surely come to understand how similar values can diverge greatly when influenced by different life experiences and sources of information. I began to understand that we all carry with us needs and fears that can shape our perceptions so that what looks like "right" to one person can be "wrong" to another. Much of the support for the war was based on values and concerns like my Dad's—values not that different from my own. I could see the threads that joined us, and the differences as well. Usually the differences dominated the actions of both sides. But did that have to always be the case?

I first encountered the practice of active listening while working as a counselor with troubled adolescents in a group home in Vermont. The Mountain Road School and Group Home staff not only listened to the kids, we also gave them opportunities to reflect on troublesome issues and help make decisions and find solutions. These were kids who were hurting emotionally and then reacting negatively to the point where they had to be removed from their homes and placed in a therapeutic environment. They were failing in many areas of life. Yet when we held group meetings, their voices were encouraged, heard, and respected. The result was that they were sometimes able to reflect and self-examine. They revealed their inner pain and fears as well as their desires and ideas for positive change. In other words, many of the solutions were inside these kids who were often seen as "delinquents" or "victims." Through active listening, their wisdom and insights became a primary part of the group home's therapeutic environment.

In the late 1970's I began once again to work for social change. Each time I applied listening and empathy to whatever I was doing, I was amazed at how it reduced people's defensiveness. I could see that so often defensiveness, including my own, was what crippled people's ability to consider other ideas and possibilities. Asking questions and listening, on the other hand, reduced and even eliminated defensiveness. Especially when I listened not just for the words a person said, but also for the underlying feelings and needs that I could more easily understand. This was the kind of listening we had used at the Mountain Road Group Home. It was the kind of listening that could, and eventually did, help me understand the fears, hopes, needs, and concerns of the whole person – including our differences, and our common ground.

In 1981, my wife Marnie and I were teaching at the Arthur Morgan School in rural North Carolina. At that time, a relatively small number of social change groups in the rural southeast U.S. were working on various local, regional, and national issues. Some good things were happening but most groups were somewhat isolated and discouraged by local opposition or apathy. As one person put it, "Often we are seen as troublemakers or outsiders."

At that time, I too was frustrated by local and regional resistance to change on important issues of justice, health, education, conflict, and the environment. So I decided to publish a newsletter that featured the voices of people and groups in the region who were creatively and effectively responding to local, regional, and national issues. The newsletter was **Rural Southern Voice for Peace (RSVP).** After several years as editor with a wonderful group of dedicated volunteers, we were able to hire a skilled staff to manage the newsletter. I use the word "hire" lightly, for we were all working at below minimum wage.

The RSVP newsletter and my travels in the southeast region of the country soon gave rise to a vibrant network of individuals and grassroots organizations sharing information, inspiration, and resources on working effectively for positive, community-based change. The newsletter was written by our readers, who were in rural communities where what you say and do has immediate consequences. If not sensitive to other people's ideas, beliefs, and needs, you wouldn't necessarily get run out of town, but you would soon be ineffectively spinning your wheels and preaching to the choir. That knowledge pointed me in the direction of community organizing that is rooted in listening to individuals and communities in a manner that can reveal creative community-based solutions and leadership. Listening to perceived opponents could be a cornerstone to effective community education and action.

During my visits with our slowly-but-steadily-growing RSVP community in the southeastern U.S., I also saw the need for a more comprehensive organizing and action process that was based on building bridges to people with different or opposing views. I wanted to get beyond the "conservative" and "liberal" labels that so often divide us.

The first event that was called a Community Listening Project took place in the fall of 1983, but prior to that I did trial runs applying listening in a more structured way. For example, I went to a Yancey County Health Fair and asked my rural, southern Appalachian neighbors questions about national security, health, and the nuclear arms race - which at this time was a divisive issue. The responses came from people who had never before been given the opportunity to respond to well-crafted, respectful questions that simply provided them with an opportunity to reflect on the reality of nuclear weapons and the possibility of nuclear war. I gave them time to reflect on a proposal for a nuclear freeze that would allow the U.S. and the U.S.S.R. to stop building any more nuclear weapons. The responses from those whom we interviewed revealed support for an adequate national defense and a preference for achieving national security without nuclear weapons.

An early local project influenced our county government to create the county's first-ever recycling program, and another one empowered our health department to create new support systems for nursing mothers, including work-site breast pumps so working mothers did not have to stop nursing their infants. Coming up are stories of Listening Projects that have changed the lives of individuals and communities throughout the U.S. and internationally.

I have been blessed with the opportunity to engage in many Listening Projects, as a participant or a trainer. At the same time, I've had plenty of times in my personal life where I have been a poor listener, reacting with fear or self-interest. We've all had such experiences. The thing about listening, though, is that there are so many opportunities to learn and fail and learn again—from neighbors, family, friends, and especially from the people with whom we experience conflict. As we keep trying and learning and getting it right, we can accomplish much with the understanding, compassion, and commitment that can grow within us through the simple but profound art of listening.

Chapter 3

Listening in the Family: One Mother's Story

~ Narrative by Donna O'Toole

This very personal story is here at the front of the book because it's a good reminder that social change starts with personal change. Every day we have many opportunities to listen in a way that can change our lives.

Late on the night of my son Matt's 16th birthday, he came into the kitchen as I was washing dishes. He was, he said, unable to sleep. Nothing new, I thought. Matt had Cystic Fibrosis, a serious and chronic lung disease. He often had difficulty sleeping. At the time, children diagnosed with cystic fibrosis seldom lived past eighteen years, and Matt knew his infant sister had died of the same disease. His lung capacity compromised, he couldn't run and play Little League baseball like other kids, but he did his best to live with what he had.

Earlier that evening, Matt had told me how much he disliked it when people bought gifts for someone they really didn't know, just because it was their birthday. Then he told me how much he liked the poem I had written for him and the homemade card I had given him for this birthday.

As Matt continued speaking, his voice grew louder and increasingly agitated. He talked about the importance of people sharing what is real and honest, but said most people won't do that, because they were artificial. He spoke with disgust and anger about phony people in his school and in our church community.

It was very hard for me to listen to him. I wanted to say something that might help calm, comfort, or quiet him. I thought, "I'm his mother, I should be doing more than just listening." Matt was so obviously distraught; his anger was elevating and so was my fear.

Could my son really stand the mental anguish he was expressing? Could I? I knew there was more going on here than anger at others.

But I sat down beside him and somehow kept listening. He said the teachings of the church were stupid and cruel. "Where do they get all their answers on how to live a beautiful long life?" he asked. "They think they're so goddamned smart; how in the hell do they know what it's like to be different?" I really didn't want to hear anymore. I felt ill inside. What if he mentally broke down, right in front of me? Scared but determined, I continued to listen.

Unexpectedly, Matt stopped shouting and began crying and pounding the table so hard I was afraid he'd hurt either himself or me. Still, I listened as he poured out more. Suddenly his tears turned to sobs as he blurted out, "I'm afraid to die, I don't want to die!" Shaking, he dropped his head into his arms, as he slid off the chair onto the floor. I moved to the floor, too, and took him into my arms. We cried together. After what seemed like a lifetime of silence, Matt finally lifted his head. He looked at me with a slight smile and said, "I had to say that, Mom. Thanks for listening. Now let's get those dishes done." I was shaken with the stark beauty of our exchange.

Matt lived another five years sharing feelings and articulating his wants and needs to many people. Both of us became consummate listeners. Just days before he died, he told me that, although he knew I would like him to talk with me about dying, he would not be doing so. "Mom," he said, "I only have so much air left in my lungs. I want to use every breath I have to keep living." I cried, but I listened.

Chapter 4

Listening in on a Listening Project Interview: The Louisiana Racial Issues Project

~ *Narrative by Herb Walters*

In 1989, white supremacist David Duke wins election to the Louisiana House of Representatives. In 1991 he makes an unsuccessful run for the governor's office. That same year a group of Los Angeles police officers badly beat Rodney King, an American construction worker nationally known after being beaten by Los Angeles Police Department officers. Racism and the Nazi party are enjoying attention, and they both appear to be on the ascendancy in America.

In 1992, in the town of Denham Springs, Louisiana, two men approach a small house in a mostly white, working-class neighborhood. Denham Springs is in Livingston Parish, the home of David Duke. The two men knock on the door. It is answered by Jeff, a bare-chested young man, who somewhat suspiciously regards his visitors. They introduce themselves and explain that they are conducting a survey in the neighborhood, wondering what folks have to say about racial issues. They tell Jeff that if he has some time, they'd appreciate listening to what he has to say. He nods his acceptance and leads his visitors into the living room. The following account was later written by one of the interviewers.

Jeff lights a cigarette, and from behind tired eyes says he'd been at a party until late the previous night. He seems rather wary of us, but also appears relaxed. We ask him a few preliminary questions about himself, mostly to establish a little rapport. Then we move slowly into the issue of race, first asking what he thinks are important local and national issues. Starting this way gives Jeff a chance to see that we are interested in him and really came to listen to what he has to say.

After the preliminaries, we get into the core of our interview. We ask Jeff, "What are your hopes and fears about race relations today?" His eyes narrow a little and he responds, "I think it's hopeless. I'm not a racist or anything, but Abe Lincoln should have sent them niggers back to Africa. There's such a gap between blacks and whites," Jeff continues. "We just don't understand each other."

Our training has prepared us for such statements, so we ask a clarifying question: "Why do you think that is? Why is there such a gap?"

"They're not developed like we are," he answers. "When you drive through there" (pointing in the direction of a nearby black community) "it's like going into Africa. It really is."

"What has helped create such conditions in the black community?" I ask. "Is it just because they're black, or are there other reasons?"

"Their environment affects them a lot," Jeff answers, after a slight pause. "They don't want to work. Most black people are poor. They need to get off welfare. I worked for what I have, and they could work hard and make it too, if they wanted to."

"We've got a question a little later on that asks about people trying to get off of welfare, but also finding many obstacles in their way," says my partner, Scott. "Do you know any black people who are trying to get off of welfare?"

Jeff talks about a black woman he knows who is trying to improve her situation. "She really wants to work," he says. "Sometimes she comes and uses our phone and I know she'd like to work, but you know, it's hard having kids and trying to find a decent job." He adds, "One of the problems is that so many of 'em down there are strung out on drugs."

A little later in the interview we ask, "How do your religious or moral beliefs affect your views on race?" Jeff shares some positive thoughts about everyone being equal. He then adds a comment against interracial marriages, and he says that Christians should not

20

marry non-Christians. When I ask him if interfaith or interracial marriages should be against the law, he says no, that's going too far. "The Bible is against it, but it's a free country," he said. "People can do what they want."

One of our questions is about the Los Angeles riots and the beating of Rodney King. Jeff says he thinks the beating was wrong, but that the riots were wrong, too. When we ask him about conditions in Los Angeles that may have led to the anger, frustration, and riots, he says he doesn't know much about the conditions in Los Angeles, but that the rioters lost the respect of the nation by doing what they did. He is surprised to learn from us that a significant number of whites and Latinos were also arrested for rioting.

When we started asking questions, Jeff was tense and suspicious of our intent. About 20 minutes into our interview, we noticed a significant shift. Jeff was more relaxed. He gradually realized that we were serious about listening to him. In fact, with many of his responses, we asked follow-up questions because we were genuinely interested in understanding his deeper thoughts and feelings. Jeff began to take more time to reflect and explore his feelings and ideas.

He tells us that racial tensions exist in Baton Rouge because blacks resent the fact that whites have more. His opinion softens a little when one of our interview questions reveals significant economic differences between blacks and whites. We ask him what he thinks and feels about those differences. (At that time, black unemployment was three times that of white unemployment, and over 43 percent of African American children were living in poverty.)

"It's partially racial," he says. "You shouldn't hire a black man just because he's black. But if he's qualified, hire him." He pauses and then shares with us that where he works, a black man doing the same job he does receives $3- $4 less per hour. "That's not fair," he says. "Blacks are almost still in slavery a little."

Step by step, our questions about Jeff's personal relationship with specific black people and our willingness to non-judgmentally stay with him help him open up and take another look at his attitude on race issues. We ask him to share more about the African-American woman he knows who is trying to get off welfare. He says that he respects this woman (whom we will call Sylvia). He says that he and his wife let Sylvia use their phone because she can't afford one. By talking about Sylvia's situation—the need for a phone, the lack of a car for transportation, and the need for health insurance for her children—Jeff opens to the difficulties faced by people trying to find work.

"Why do you think," we ask, "there is a perception by many people that white workers are losing ground because of affirmative action, when studies in fact show that whites have an overwhelming advantage?" Jeff's answer is frank: "The government wants to make it look like they're helping blacks, but they're really not."

Our questions about the future outlook for black children bring an unexpected response. Jeff doesn't see much of a future for them. "Growing up in poverty is the biggest factor influencing their situation," he says.

At one point, we were joined by Jeff's wife (whom we will call Wanda). Wanda gets interested in the interview and wanders in and out of the living room. She begins to add her responses to our questions. She identifies quite closely with the black woman who is trying to find work.

As we get further into the interview, we find that both Jeff and Wanda are still feeling the sting of the troubled economy. They feel that instances of corporate abuse, such as the savings and loan collapse, were critical factors in bringing about the economic problems they are experiencing today. When we ask Jeff and Wanda if they see a tendency to try to blame the poor for the country's problems, they say they do. Like most other respondents to our survey, they feel that the gap between rich and poor is growing and that the poor are being blamed for creating their own problems.

Our final questions focus on possible solutions and how Jeff and Wanda might get involved in learning more or working with others to make race relations better. Jeff's responses are very different from when we began. Racial quotas are still an unacceptable idea to him, but he says he could support other programs and affirmative action efforts if they "really help people out." "We need to be able to see concrete results right here in the black community within a year," he says. "But people need to be responsible and know how to use these programs right."

When we ask for other ideas he or Wanda might have, Jeff suggests that black people need more access to a decent education. He adds, "poor people need help with transportation to help them get to opportunities."

Wanda recalls that if her great-granddad saw a black man walking down his road, he would chase him to the far side. "There's a lot of subconscious racism around here… it's embedded in people," she says.

Both of them say they are interested in more information and in talking to others about the issues we've just discussed. "One thing we could do is come together and form a Neighborhood Watch group that could help everyone," says Wanda. Jeff agrees.

PART II

A Community Listening Project:

How It Works

> "I no longer was all alone; I was talking to people who were describing the same things that I felt. That was a very healing experience for me. I came back feeling uplifted, knowing that I had given people a gift of spending time to listen to them. In the process, I had been given a lot, too."

Chapter 5

Organizing a Community Listening Project

Listening Projects (LP's) always address local issues, and some also address regional or even national or international issues. The heart of any Listening Project is when one or more community organizations come together to identify or respond to community-based concerns, needs, or problems.

A significant amount of time is given by these organizations to determine the goals and resources that will be needed to complete a project. This is important so that an organization does not spend lots of time developing a project without clear, realistic goals or adequate resources for completion.

After developing goals, resources, and logistics for the project, listening teams of two are trained by an experienced Listening Project trainer to listen to particular neighborhoods, groups, or individuals. Each interview is conducted by an interviewer and a scribe. The interviewer uses a carefully-prepared series of questions. These non-threatening, open-ended questions give structure to the interviews, as well as keep the focus on the community's concerns and the organization's goals. (Examples of goals are in the Appendix.) Interviews are not limited, however, to only the pre-planned questions. Interviewers are trained in the art of asking follow-up questions that help the interviewee open up and investigate their deeper feelings, values, and beliefs. This keeps the process flexible and encourages a sincere exploration of the issues through respectful listening and dialogue. New ideas and solutions often emerge from this creative engagement. Interviews are generally conducted in people's homes or any place where they feel comfortable.

LP interviewers are trained in active listening because they really want to hear what people truly think and feel about concerns or issues important to the community. The listeners, of course, have their own ideas about the need for change, but they understand that an inclusive process is necessary. Subtly coercing someone to change can seem to be effective, but that kind of change is short-lived because people revert to their original beliefs. In a LP interview, we seek to provide an environment where differing sides can explore the issues in an atmosphere of mutual respect that encourages the generation of creative ideas and solutions. This caring, respectful environment helps eliminate the conflict that often gets in the way of positive change. The process empowers people to work together to find practical solutions that will be good for the community as a whole.

By conducting the interviews, organizations establish positive relations with the people they have interviewed. They gain a better understanding of the community, enabling them to more effectively work towards their goals—or change their goals if appropriate. The process stimulates creativity, identifies new resources, finds potential allies, and encourages new grassroots leadership. This last step—finding leaders within the community—broadens and strengthens organizations. The results of the interviews can be used to educate both the wider community and the initiating organization.

Chapter 6

Listening Project Results

Since 1985, Listening Projects have been used in hundreds of communities where conflict or disempowerment weakens efforts for positive change. Listening Projects have helped people and organizations successfully address issues including injustice, conflict, community development, health, and the environment. These projects have occurred throughout the U.S. as well as internationally.

Conducting a Listening Project takes a lot of time and resources but it's really worth it. It's like taking time to build the foundation of a house. Having a strong base for positive change can be built on a foundation using bricks that:

- Promote insight, empathy, and understanding among people with conflicting views
- Identify problems and issues that people care about
- Include often unheard or unheeded voices
- Foster the emergence and development of new community leaders
- Generate creative solutions for community needs and problems
- Disseminate issue-related information and determine needs for additional information
- Encourage personal growth as the people involved consider new viewpoints and information
- Form uncommon coalitions and alliances through which diverse viewpoints can be understood—rather than fought over
- Create long-term capacity for cooperative community action

Chapter 7

Listeners' Experiences

The Listening Project is grounded in the belief that the key to social change lies in our ability to communicate with open hearts and minds, bringing out the best of human nature. Thus the Listening Project is about social change that is rooted in personal change. In the process of conducting a Listening Project, personal change transforms the people being listened to, as well as the listeners.

The following quotes were gathered from listeners with the Piedmont Peace Center (PPC), based in Kannapolis, NC. The organization was founded in the early 80's by Linda Stout, as an organization of working-class people trying to reduce excessive military spending and focus more resources on human needs. PPC conducted one of the earliest Listening Projects. It was able to significantly improve the lives of the people and affect national policy on government funding priorities. Below are some reflections from different listeners who participated in the project. More information on this project can be found in **Part Three** of this book.

- *"I can't say that I joined the Listening Project just to go out and talk to everybody. I felt a lot of dread. I felt sure we were going to be shut out... Those fears never developed, however. When I got out in the neighborhood and started knocking on doors, I found that people were responsive to us."*

- *"I had a wonderful experience with one woman I talked to. Just like during the training, she shared very intimate parts of her life, describing that she'd never finished high school and had gone back as an adult to get her GED, and what that meant to her. She described how important she felt education was and how concerned she was that the government was spending money on missiles and on war, without enough regard for children or for people who were homeless. She offered all this information even before we got to our questions about military spending. She made all the connections herself. I was soothed by this woman's eloquence. That happened over and over again during our interviews. It made me feel that this Listening Project was the right thing to do. I saw that people really need more information. We need to have a way to talk about these problems."*

- *"People often would follow us out the door and onto the porch. I felt like I'd just made a friend. They directed me to other neighbors down the street. It left me feeling what a gift the whole experience is. I was really struck by that. It really is a powerful feeling to have someone tell you that they really care about what you think."*

- *"Another thing I learned was how truly powerless some people feel. A lot of the people that I talked with—I would say the majority of them—didn't vote, weren't registered, and didn't even know where to go to register. I felt connected with them and it gave me a real sense of sadness, because they felt that there was nothing they could do. But I think that we take the first step when we sit down and talk with someone and bring out the emotions and concerns that are inside. When we get someone to realize that they are really being listened to, they'll say, 'Yeah, I really think this is wrong. I may not understand the problems perfectly, but I think it's wrong and I need to tell somebody about it.' Later it felt very good when we helped these people register to vote and many of them got involved in working to make changes."*

- *"When we asked the question about what she would do if she were President—what kind of changes would she make—she said, 'I just can't even imagine that. That is beyond me. I can't think about it.' But then I asked, 'Just think about it for a minute. Talk about some of the issues you are concerned about. What would you do to change them?' She paused for a minute and just started naming all these ideas. I said, 'Those are great ideas!' I felt over and over how special people are, and so often we don't even see it. I know that people who come from a lower income background are simply forgotten by the system.*

But I saw how really special they are, and how much our society misses by not getting a chance to see what is inside them. What kind of changes do you think need to be made? People aren't asked that question enough.

- *"Not everything I heard was to my liking, but the thing I did learn—and we talked about this in the training—is that some people may come out with a remark that we feel is offensive. But I found out that there really is a story behind these statements, and it was nice to be able to remember that. Sometimes there were areas where I just couldn't agree with someone, but we were still able to find some common ground."*

Part III

Listening Project Stories

> "I had never thought of myself as an activist. I didn't start out with that goal for my life. People were just showing up at my door all day and into the night, bringing their empty water jugs and their fears, their questions, and frustrations all rolled into their stories."

Chapter 8

Toxic Waste in Appalachia: The Harlan County Listening Project

~ *Narrative by Theresa Osborne*

Harlan County, Kentucky is in the far eastern corner of the state, deep in southern Appalachian coal country. The many small communities that sit in the shadow of the mountains have historically been exploited countless times by large corporate interests. The Dayhoit community of Harlan County is one such place.

We begin with the voice of Joan Robinett:

Dear God, they have poisoned my child! I lie awake at night, unable to sleep with that thought rolling around in my head like a chorus of accusations. They poisoned my child. They poisoned my child. Oh Lord, I poisoned my child.

I gave him drinks of water before bedtime and drew his bubble baths. I sprayed him and his friends with the water hose on hot summer days; I filled his wading pool with that water. I poisoned my child.

No, wait. Wait a minute. I didn't know. They didn't tell me. They probably would never have told me. They poisoned my child.

It's been 15 years. I should be able to sleep by now, but I can't. I keep thinking about it all, and playing it over and over again in my mind. Now I live in a good house on a high hill in Harlan town. At night I can look down on the city lights, and I still hear the crickets and the night birds sing. I can see the floodwall and the sparkle of the Cumberland River, sliding, rolling, lazing along beside the road as it glides right on down to Dayhoit, past the National Electric

Coil plant, the Holiday Mobile Home Park, and then on to Bowling Green.

Toxic chemicals. Who thinks about toxic chemicals, for God's sake? This is Harlan County, Kentucky. Everywhere you look there are beautiful big green mountains. Some people say they isolate us from the rest of the world. They say that Pine Mountain and Black Mountain are just big green walls that have kept out the world, as well as progress, and money, and people. Some folks say we ought to be blowing these mountains up to sell the coal underneath. Others say the mountains haven't kept out near enough of the world, and its progress, and money, and strangers. That our forests, our mountains and our pure clear mountain spring water are the most precious resources we have.

They poisoned my child. I keep asking myself, "How could this have happened? When did they know? Why didn't I see it?"

Trouble Appears: National Electric Coil Comes to Harlan County

In the 1950s a new company—National Electric Coil—started up in Harlan County. It rebuilt electric motors for the coal mines. The company cleaned the old grubby equipment before tearing it down by using a marvelous solvent that the plant stored in vats. Its vapors alone were able to strip the grease from the mining equipment. Joan Robinett remembers employees carrying the solvent home in bottles, to clean up dirty clothes, stained hands, and even whitewall tires. Some folks seemed leery of the solvent, but the plant owners never let on that it might be harmful.

Next to the plant was an old drive-in theater that a Cumberland River flood destroyed in 1977. Joan recalls:

They decided not to re-build the drive-in. Instead, they drilled a well to supply water and turned the spot into a trailer court: Holiday Mobile Home Park. They put up a fence at the edge of the park. I guess it was to keep the kids off the NEC property. It didn't matter; they played in the vacant field anyway.

It was business as usual. People moved into the trailer park, and no one thought about the factory less than 100 yards away, except maybe when they went outside and saw the sticky yellow film on their cars and on the outside of their trailers. Then a wife would ask her husband, or a friend who worked in the plant, to bring home some of that "good cleaner" so they could wash the trailer and the car, as well as the greasy cabinets and stained clothes. I wonder... did the owners of the plant know then?

My husband and I, with our healthy little boy, Dan, moved to Dayhoit and into the Holiday Mobile Home Park in 1984. Well, he was healthy... until after we moved there. All the kids were sick. They were always passing things back and forth: stomach flu, diarrhea. But Dan really got sick. We even had to air-evac him to the big hospital in Cincinnati a couple of times. It was a scary time, because the doctors could never figure out what caused Dan to be so sick. Why didn't I see it? It is so obvious now, looking back.

We moved on up the river about three miles to Rio Vista in 1988. Whatever had been wrong with Dan got better and seemed to go away. We were so glad.

EPA Enters the Picture

In 1989, the EPA showed up to test the well that supplied the water to Holiday Mobile Home Park. Shortly thereafter residents of Dayhoit received the following notice: "Due to organic chemicals found in the well water supply... the Division of Water has placed a ban on consuming water from this supply... residents [should] not use the water for bathing or showering."

Vinyl chloride from an "unidentified source" had contaminated the area's groundwater, and residents would not ever be able to flush their wells clean. Residents were further advised that boiling the water was not only ineffective, but dangerous. After issuing this warning about the water that people had been using for years, these same officials stated that the risk to people's health was small.

Vinyl chloride had been used there since the plant was built in 1950. At an early public meeting, the state of Kentucky claimed it had not even known of the existence of National Electric Coil (NEC) until 1987. In the fall of 1989, National Electric Coil refused to allow the state to test its soil.

While the polluting company did not admit liability or complicity, it did confirm finding "trace amounts" of the chemicals. With great public hoopla and amazing swiftness, the company announced that it would fund the design and construction of an extension of the county water system to the affected part of the community. At the Holiday Mobile Home Park, the new water lines stopped at the entrance and were simply coupled to the old lines that had carried poisoned water for over thirty years. Besides having untested residual contamination, these pipes were so corroded that the trailer court residents were given notice to boil their city-supplied water. Adding insult to injury, the residents were forced to pay a steep price for water that formerly came from their own wells. Many residents lived on fixed incomes and were unable to pay the water bills.

Then the Kentucky division of water came in and held two or three public meetings. At one of the meetings, a state expert said, "We found cancer-causing chemicals in the drinking water at the mobile home park and some other wells close by, but your chances of getting cancer are very slim. However, do not drink this water. Do not wash your clothes, water your lawns, do not do anything with this water."

Joan Robinett speaks about the contaminated water:

When their well was shut off, my friends from the mobile home park came to my house to get water in gallon plastic milk jugs. They were being provided two gallons of water a day by the authorities. But if they wanted more, they would come to my house to get water. We sat around my kitchen table and began to talk about our kids, about the constant stomach flus and stuff that they all supposedly had. Their kids were sick a lot. Mine had been too. Until we started to sit around my kitchen table and talk, we didn't realize that everybody's kids were sick.

I was thinking, "Okay, it's cancer-causing chemicals. They say our chances of getting cancer are slim. But these people say we can't ever use this water again. Something is not right here."

So I called my son's gastro-neurologist at the University of Cincinnati Children's Hospital. I told him what we knew and the names of the chemicals that had been found in the drinking water, where we had lived at the time Dan was coming to the hospital up there. His response was 'Oh, my God.' Yeah. O my God, I thought. They have poisoned my child—and her child... and her child... and how many other children? They have poisoned our community!

The people kept on showing up at my house, to fill their water jugs and sit at my kitchen table to talk. Workers at the plant showed up at my table to tell their stories. They told about following a company policy that had them empty the degreasing pits by spilling the contents onto the ground around the plant. When the earth became saturated, the chemicals were dumped directly into the Cumberland River, behind the plant. Degreaser and transformer oil was also used to kill weeds along the factory's chain-link fence. The workers were instructed to burn PCB-laden electrical transformers. They did this late at night because open burning was illegal. The worst contamination to the workers occurred once a week when the tanks were cleaned. A worker had to crawl into the degreasing tank – and then get back out within three to five minutes – before blacking out. The entire cleaning process took up to four hours. Not one former worker reported being informed by management of the harmful effects of any of the toxic chemicals they used daily.

The plant had sunk wells that they filled with used chemicals, which made their way into the aquifer. They had dumped chemicals on the vacant field outside the plant. They burned some, hauled some off to the landfill, and sometimes they just opened the drain plugs and let the stuff run into the river.

Citizens Organize and Take Action

In January 1990, NEC presented its "clean-up plan" to the state's environmental agency. At the same time, they hired a public

36

relations firm to produce a full page newspaper ad that claimed, "There is absolutely no cause for concern about the possibility of exposure to any of the chemicals." Included in the ad were supportive statements made by toxicologists from the University of Louisville who had been hired by the company.

The state itself, in fact, became dependent upon the tests taken by the company. Robinett articulated citizens' frustration when she said: "The state wants us to depend [for the test results] on the same people who poisoned us!" But because of the state's inaction, in July of 1990, the federal Environmental Protection Agency (EPA) became the primary governmental agency responsible for supervision of the clean-up in Dayhoit. EPA contemplated placing the NEC site on the "Superfund" list. The citizens viewed the EPA's entrance with mixed emotions. Although the EPA had more resources, they were also more remote, and their involvement would mean further delay. Superfund clean-up could not begin before 1994, and residents didn't want to endure contamination for another three years while EPA decided what it wanted to do.

When direct questions were evaded—and laboratories delayed or "lost" the results of water tests—residents realized that they had to take action themselves. They formed Concerned Citizens against Toxic Waste (CCATW) and held a rally that drew 75 people. The group held elections, collected dues, and named a steering committee. By this time, they realized that the state's strategy was: "If we don't tell them anything, they won't know anything."

By pooling what they learned from trips to libraries and visits with state offices, and by contracting independent testing, the group soon discovered that the extent of the poisoning was greater than they had feared. Fourteen poisonous chemicals—including mercury, lead, arsenic, naphthalene, polychlorinated biphenyls (PCBs), trichloroethylene (TCE), chlorinated solvents, asbestos, epoxy resins, and silica—were found at toxic levels in the soil and water of Dayhoit. A preliminary health survey of Dayhoit residents, arranged by CCATW, found high incidence of respiratory problems, skin irritations, nerve disorders, and kidney and liver disease.

When NEC company began removing truckloads of dirt from around the factory, CCATW suspected the removal was an attempt to remove the evidence before a thorough evaluation could be made. CCATW put up a picket line that was honored by truckers. The soil removal stopped and within a week NEC agreed to test the soil. This was CCATW's first victory. One lesson they learned was how sensitive the polluters were to public exposure.

CCATW then pressured the company to pay for a health assessment. After examining a number of former workers, a doctor recommended that all former workers should be tested annually for the rest of their lives to detect the expected development of diseases such as leukemia and liver cancer. Unfortunately, CCATW discovered that much of the allotted half million dollars disappeared into a pork barrel for the county. $6,000, for instance, went to a local fire department for the one-day use of their truck to haul water.

Joan talks about becoming an activist:

We organized. We started the group Concerned Citizens Against Toxic Waste. I was elected Chairman. So now I was a community leader, an activist... or that nosey bitch stirring up trouble down at Dayhoit. I had never thought of myself as an activist. I didn't start out with that goal for my life. People were just showing up at my door all day and into the night, bringing their empty water jugs and their fears, their questions, and frustrations all rolled into their stories.

How bad was the pollution? "Why, I have eaten fish out of that river for 20 years. That's where my son caught his first fish."

Was it in the soil and could it get into our food? "Well, Mr. Jones doesn't live in the trailer park, but his place is right next door, and he's got a well, too. He's lived there for years. I remember during the '77 flood he had to leave his house because the water got up..."

How many people were sick and how many might get sick later? "You know I've got this rash. It started about two years after I started working at NEC. I just got up one morning..."

And we all wanted to know, how could we fix this? Could it be fixed? And who was going to be held responsible?

They came to my house because I had water. We started talking because I had lived in that trailer park and I had the same fears and questions they did. I kept thinking that what has happened to all of us is wrong, and somebody in the government will fix this and make it right for us. It didn't take long to realize I was wrong about that. I wanted to help. I wanted to do something. I couldn't sit around and wait until this got swept under the rug. So I became an activist. I learned right away that I had a lot to learn.

Enter the Listening Project

Concerned Citizens Against Toxic Waste was making some headway, but there was still a long way to go. The group made contact with several public interest groups, most helpful of which was the Highlander Center in New Market, Tennessee. After attending a Save the Planet/ Stop the Poisoning workshop at Highlander Center, CCATW decided to conduct a survey to discover the full extent of the damage to residents' health.

Having met some of the CCATW members at a workshop, Listening Project RSVP contacted the group and suggested that the survey they were considering might be expanded into a Listening Project. Listening Project RSVP suggested that rather than simply documenting disease and disorder in their community, the group could use a Listening Project to expand their work and go on to (1) educate the community on the issue, (2) ask residents for their ideas and solutions, (3) overcome some residents' fears about getting involved, (4) identify new leaders, and (5) promote CCATW's efforts to the general public. In short, a Listening Project could bring the wider community together and galvanize them to take specific actions that federal and state officials were slow to do.

Many residents were concerned about taking action against any company that provided jobs where so few were available. Listening Project RSVP staff heard, "People around here are afraid to speak out. Here the coal companies have held power, and people are used to being under the thumb of the company store." Although this came from a former worker at the factory, CCATW was nonetheless enthusiastic about expanding the scope of their project. As Listening Project RSVP helped formulate the survey questions for the Dayhoit Listening Project, it became evident that CCATW had already laid much of the groundwork. The members of CCATW were dedicated not only to a clean environment but also to justice for residents who had been slowly poisoned for decades.

After several months of consultation and preparation, the day came for Listening Project RSVP to give the training to the two dozen volunteer listeners assembled by CCATW. All of them were locals who knew each other and were connected to the pollution at Dayhoit, either by association with workers or by having lived in the neighborhood. Some of them were so angry at having been treated poorly by government that it was all RSVP could do, as trainers, to keep them focused on the task of listening. Some of them wanted to bang on doors and shout answers!

CCATW wanted to find out whether every well had been tested, and they wanted to thoroughly document the actual effects on residents' health, so the group decided to talk to every household in the community. Listening Project RSVP explained that, even though the area was not heavily populated, their goal of interviewing everyone might be too ambitious, since the Listening Project technique requires more time and involvement with individuals than a standard checklist survey. But the group was clear that they wanted to talk to everybody; and although it took them several months, they interviewed just about the entire community.

When the LP got underway, instead of finding closed doors, or fear or hostility, CCATW found support and welcome. As Joan put it: "We'd never had a chance before to touch base with all the people here in Dayhoit. The Listening Project helped people bring out things that normally they won't talk about. It was a great chance to understand their feelings and find out what the confusion and fears were."

Joan's account of the Listening Project:

A lot of people were afraid to speak out on their own, so we wanted to gather their stories. We organized our Listening Project and we began going to people's houses to sit at their kitchen tables and hear their stories.

We heard about the boy whose family lives up the river, but he spent every afternoon after school and all summer with his grandmother in Dayhoit. Now he has cancer. We heard gardening stories, and fishing stories, and swimming-in-the-river stories, and who lived where, who visited who, and how they all were all connected together by this now-toxic aquifer.

With all our listening, people started understanding better what was going on, and plenty of them started thinking that maybe they could help do something about it. Now more folks were willing to start speaking out and they came to our meetings and got involved in our health studies. The listening got nearly the whole community stirred up and we got plenty of ideas about how CCATW could continue our fight for justice.

Listening Project trainer Herb Walters found that several of the people he helped interview hadn't made the connection between their own health problems and the chemical contamination of the community. "One woman sat and responded calmly to our questions," Herb reported. "Then about halfway through, she began talking about her child's recurring stomach problems that the doctors couldn't explain. I could just see her spark with a new realization: 'I think maybe this chemical poisoning could be causing all these problems,' she said."

After knocking on over one hundred doors, CCATW found itself with a different kind of problem—a desirable one. As Joan said, "We found out people are really willing to help. We had lots of new people offer to help us. We had to be creative now about finding ways to involve these new people! In the past, I would have assumed that someone, somewhere, in government would have done something. Now, I don't assume anything."

The Aftermath

The Dayhoit Listening Project also met the original intention of the group: to document health disorders. Using a computer program donated by the local community college, some of the findings were transformed into traditional pie charts. The survey documented which wells had been tested and uncovered the fact that some wells had been tested only for bacteria—not for the chemicals responsible for the poisonings. Another unexpected finding was the presence of a large number of people with learning problems; so attention was directed toward the relationship between learning problems and lead contamination. In midsummer of 1990, CCATW initiated, at their own expense, the testing for lead in people's blood samples. CCATW reports that this medically supervised study was made much easier because of the community contact initially made through the Listening Project.

CCATW also received a $10,000 grant that they applied to a successful kidney study. This analysis revealed the level of toxic chemicals that residents and former workers had been exposed to. CCATW referred to this as the "Pee for Justice" campaign!

CCATW was eventually successful with its four goals: (1) to have thorough testing of the area's groundwater, (2) to have thorough testing of the soil and the Cumberland River floodplain, (3) to have free comprehensive medical testing for all those affected, and (4) to have citizen input and evaluation of the cleanup plan.

Joan reflects on the settlement:

Eventually we filed a court case and told our stories in court. We told about the drive-in movie with the contaminated soil, the diseased fish in the river, the floodwaters that spread contamination so effectively that we don't even want to think about it. We told about the health problems we have now, and the problems we are afraid we may have in the future. Those stories helped us win a multi-million-dollar compensation settlement and an additional settlement for a future cancer fund, available to any of the 550 people who were part of that lawsuit.

If they develop particular types of cancer in the future, they will be compensated again. They don't have to hire an attorney; they don't have to go back into court. If they're diagnosed, their doctor can send a pathology report to an accounting firm, and after they confirm the diagnosis, the fund writes the person a check. You can't replace someone's life with money, no matter what, but the money will help.

I heard a story about how the fund paid for hotel rooms, food, gas, and time off from work, so a mother could have her husband and children with her through her cancer treatments. She died, but her family at least was able to be with her.

In November of 1996, after months of trial and two days before the jury was to begin deliberating, the case was settled. Clearly, the Federal superfund status impacted the company's decision to settle the cases before the jury could give a verdict. Since this all began, I have learned about open-record laws, contaminant particles, gag orders, the politics of profit, and how to stand up for myself and what I believe in. I have been to Washington and met a President. I am called a political activist. I used to be just a housewife and mom, but the people of Dayhoit and their stories changed all that. I couldn't just sit there and listen without doing something. Someone had to do something.

Now, I lie here awake at night and go over and over the stories in my mind. On those nights when I can't sleep, maybe unconsciously I am waiting for the phone to ring. When it does, will it be another of my friends from Dayhoit calling to tell me their doctor has given them a diagnosis that makes them eligible for that fund, a kind of lottery winner of death? I have gotten a lot of those calls over the years. There have been more than I want to think about, and I still can't help remembering each one of the stories. Remembering their stories keeps me from thinking of my own story that doesn't have an end yet.

My son is now in college and has won a prestigious internship. I am so very proud of him. But, when the phone rings, and I know it's him, my heart freezes just for a second. We lived in that trailer park for three years. Is he all right? Am I?

43

There have been moments that I wanted revenge, but I don't think I'll get it. Maybe if we keep listening and work hard enough, we will all get some justice. That is my hope. That is what gets me up in the morning after I lie awake all night remembering the stories. That gives me the strength to drive to one more house, to sit and listen to the story of a mother who has lost one son to cancer and now faces losing another to the same kind of cancer, all because they lived in Dayhoit.

I knew that somebody had to do something, years ago when people started arriving at my door with their white gallon jugs, asking for water and someone to talk to. I guess to make Harlan a better place to live, then, we had to create a space where we could sit down with folks and listen to each other.

Chapter 9

Christian Stewardship of Creation

~ Narrative by Herb Walters

Yancey County is a beautiful Appalachian mountain community with two primary mountain-fed watersheds and hundreds of clear creeks and streams. The County has experienced rapid land development that has included building on steep slopes and ecologically sensitive mountaintops. Among other things, this was affecting local water quality and availability, which was also being impacted by pesticide contamination, sewage system problems, and the fact that some existing homes still straight-pipe their human waste into mountain streams. Several past efforts at county planning to address environmental concerns had continually failed due to opposition from residents who have strong feelings about property rights and "environmentalism."

The Christian Stewardship Listening Project (CSLP) began in 2007 with people from several area churches who were concerned about the county's natural resources, and they wanted to find common ground with other Christians who seemed to be disinterested or negative about environmental protection. Together they conducted a Listening Project as a means of opening dialogue on environmental concerns from a faith perspective: stewardship of God's creation.

Following several months of preparation, 6 trained interview teams went out over a period of several months to interview 28 church leaders—both pastors and laity. As is the case in most Southern Appalachian communities, most pastors hold other jobs to make ends meet. Thus CSLP interviews also revealed the reflections of working people in our county. Each interviewee was asked 21 open-ended questions about their churches and matters of faith and stewardship. Given the fact that the vast majority of churches in the county are conservative, a large majority of interviewees were likewise conservative.

Faith-Based Concerns and Home-Grown Solutions

In many cases, CSLP was interviewing people who had negative or suspicious feelings about environmental issues. Yet all their interviews were positive because they came not as advocates with an agenda, but as fellow Christians and as listeners who sincerely wanted to find out the concerns, hopes, and priorities of the people they interviewed. Interviewers didn't tell people the meaning of Creation stewardship—rather they asked them to share the meaning that they themselves found in those words – from their own life experiences. In this way, each person interviewed defined creation stewardship in Yancey County.

The following is a small sampling of responses we heard during our interviews:

- *"I remember when there were plenty of springs you could drink from. You didn't worry about what was on top of the mountains. Now many springs are gone. The mountaintops are covered with houses. The land is logged till everything is gone. I grew up logging... we were careful... we didn't take everything. Now they cut everything and there is no concern that the water will dry up without the trees."*
- *"We've always understood this land because we made our living from the land, and people know you don't cut your own throat by abusing what you need."*
- *"If we don't steward the land, so many of the experiences that I enjoyed growing up here are going to be totally gone for future generations."*
- *"A large part of being a Christian is a feeling of wonder and awe for Creation as a gift from God. Christian worship should be a part of our wonder. We must respond with gratitude and by being good caretakers."*
- *"Genesis mandates that to govern as stewards is for all of us. Sometimes we make fun of 'tree huggers' when we as Christians should be the ones supporting and leading the way."*
- *"There is no reason why we can't simultaneously have good*

jobs and protect God's creation. We need to find the right balance and continue working toward economic development that is good for both the people and the environment."

- *"The Bible says that God created the earth and it was good. So if He hadn't cared about it, He wouldn't have created it. Then Satan comes in and he says: 'Well, the only way to hurt God is to hurt what he cares about.' So he's going to hurt God's creation whether it be you and I, whether it be the animal kingdom or this earth. I believe it's a plan that he works both through the minds of people and through anything he can use."*

The listening project also enabled CSLP to identify barriers to change. One key barrier was expressed by a local pastor of an independent church:

- *"I think because environmental matters have sometimes done wrong without enough regard for the people it affects, some people react to anything environmental and throw the baby out with the bath water. In other words, they react to anything environmental even when really some things need protection. I remember when I was young things got pretty bad here. Some of the pit mines really left a mess, and the South Toe River was brown with scummy foam. It was really polluted. I'm glad it was cleaned up. I want the clean water here for my children and grandchildren. But you can't just legislate; you have to involve the people."*

Interviews with this pastor and others identified the need for increasing community participation in determining the environmental priorities and initiatives that affect people's lives. Many also identified the need for people to be better informed. When asked if churches could play a role in informing and educating people, most church leaders said yes.

CSLP education efforts began with the release of a series of articles in the local paper that shared the findings of the interviews. Generally, environmental issues are controversial in the county, but there were only positive responses to the articles because county residents could easily identify with CSLP's local, faith-based approach to environmental stewardship.

Education continued as CSLP expanded its listening through "Prayer Dialogue and Reflection" sessions that enabled church members to come together in their own church to reflect and listen to one another in both small and large groups. This enabled CSLP to further broaden faith community input into defining and identifying priorities for creation care in the county. Once again, issues of water protection and problems associated with rapid land development rose to the forefront of people's priorities.

Programs

CSLP eventually became the Christian Stewardship of Creation Project (CSCP), with a steering committee composed primarily of church leaders interviewed by the Listening Project. 2010 program work included: (1) Engaging churches in Adopt-A-Stream, which helps protect the French Broad River Basin, (2) helping churches get free energy audits, (3) identifying applicants for low-income family home weatherization provided by our local community action agency, (4) organizing a workshop on Creation Stewardship for two high school groups, and (5) founding a second organization - Sustainable Yancey.

Sustainable Yancey (SY) was started in 2009 in response to the fact that many people who were interviewed didn't trust "outsiders" or environmentalists to set the agenda for land and water protection. They wanted a "sensible" local approach to Creation care that took into account the economic and other needs of families and working people.

SY was able to build bipartisan support for sustainable development. Local government and other civic officials as well as workers and business owners have come together through the organization to develop priorities, strategies, and plans for sustainable development. Priorities established by the Christian Stewardship Listening Project provided guidance to SY program priorities. In turn, SY's influence helped inaugurate a new County

Watershed Protection Board that will review and hopefully improve county watershed regulations. We are also partners in a major effort to restore and protect both the Toe and Cane Rivers.

A Farmer, Logger and Miner and Creation Stewardship

In responding to CSLP interviews, this pastor shared some of his stories that speak eloquently about Christian stewardship and about Appalachian faith and culture.

"My maternal grandfather was a farmer, a logger, and he did a little mining... He was a man who derived his very existence from the earth... Some of the things that he demonstrated in his life were: that you didn't dig anything out of the ground unless you were going to use it, you didn't kill anything unless you were going to eat it, and you didn't chop something down unless you had a use for it. I don't think I ever saw him waste anything. He had the ability to use every part of everything. (Our ancestors) were self-sufficient, with the exception of maybe sugar and coffee and flour. They grew just about everything. So I guess one of the things he instilled in me was the fact we need to be able to know how to use what we have. But in doing that, in order to be self-sufficient and not have all the trash, you have to respect what you have. You don't waste it; you don't just misuse things.

"I remember when I was real small my Grand-dad would clear the cornfield on top of one of the mountains or ridges that he owned, and he had an old horse and a sled, and when I was small we'd get on that sled and we'd ride it up to that cornfield. I always wondered why he'd made a cornfield so remote from the rest of the farm. I mean you had to go up the side of this mountain, through woods, and finally you'd get to the top of this field. I never asked him why he'd put it up there but in thinking about it, it became pretty obvious. We'd ride up there to hoe the corn but much of the time we just sat up there and looked out over the mountains and he'd tell stories. I'd just sit there with him and we'd be looking around at the beauty of God's Creation. I was talking to him one day and he said, "Son, I'm going to give you a piece of advice,"

and I said, "What's that?" and he said, "Life's too short to spend it doing something you hate." And he said, "God put this creation here for us to enjoy and regardless of how much we have to do, don't get so busy you miss it." I've never forgotten that.

"Grand-dad taught me how to look at the things around us and tell what was going on, like, say, we're going to have a hard winter— because of the amount of mast, you know the nuts and acorns and stuff. He could look at the sky and tell what the weather was going to be. He could look at the way the smoke went up or fell down, and his weather forecasts were a lot more accurate than what we get today... And I was just completely fascinated all the years that I knew him by the wealth of knowledge this man had, and it was all from his interaction with the environment. It was all his love of nature and creation and respect for what God had entrusted to him, because he felt that the land he owned was a sacred trust. He said, 'Of course we don't own it, it's loaned to us for a while. For what time we do have jurisdiction over it, we're responsible for it.

"So I feel the same way. I know that what we have about us is for us to use, but not misuse. It's put here to sustain us and in a sense to take care of, but at the same time I believe that God expects us not to waste, not to abuse, and not to be careless with what has been created. What has been given us is so awesome and beautiful that it amazes me that people can just misuse it..."

Chapter 10:

Partners in Sustainable Agriculture

~ Narrative by Gary Gumz

In 1995, the W.K. Kellogg Foundation funded innovative Partners in Agriculture (PIA) project in North Carolina. At the time this project was initiated, the term "sustainable" was still relatively unknown. It held negative connotations for many farmers and rural folk, the suspicion being that sustainability was one of "those environmentalist ideas" that had nothing to do with the economic realities of farming. PIA was an effort to demonstrate that sustainable, environmentally-sound farming methods would benefit both the environment and the livelihood of farmers and their communities.

PIA was conducted in four regions of the state—mountains, piedmont, northern coastal plain and southern coastal plain. Four agricultural communities, one in each of these regions, were selected to participate in the project.

The project partners that directed the overall effort and provided training and resources to each community included: Carolina Farm Stewardship Association, Land Loss Prevention Project, North Carolina AT&T University, NC Coalition of Farm and Rural Families, NC State University, Rural Advancement Foundation International, and Rural Southern Voice for Peace.

Primary leadership for each project, in the form of steering committees, came from farmers, marketers, and other individuals and organizations engaged in the farm economy. The foundation for PIA was listening projects that enabled citizens in these four farm communities to set the agenda and the priorities of PIA.

Mountain Partners in Agriculture (MPIA)

Madison County and northern Buncombe County became the center of PIA work in the mountain region. Three main issues were identified from the MPIA Listening Project interviews conducted during late 1995 and early 1996. The most significant issue—according to the farmers, marketers, retailers, and community residents interviewed—was the increased pressure on farms and farmland from the cyclic effects of sprawl and increased taxes. Those interviewed felt that the best answer to this destructive cycle was an effective program of farmland protection and conservation. Recognizing the uncertain future of Burley tobacco production, local farmers also expressed concern over finding alternative cash crops and increasing farm profitability. Finally, farmers voiced the need for adding value to farm commodities, and they were particularly enthusiastic about developing specialized markets.

These issues were further explored during numerous community meetings held in 1996 and 1997. As a result of the initial survey response and continued community dialogue, the following four main goals evolved, becoming the four "Ps" that guided MPIA work:

1. Farmland **Protection**—protecting and enhancing productive farmland threatened by sprawl and scattered rural growth.
2. Marketing **Promotion**—promoting existing and establishing new marketing opportunities and cooperative ventures.
3. Sustainable **Production**—developing sustainable production systems for high-value crops and value-added commodities; and providing educational and training opportunities.
4. **Policy** Development—shaping public policies and private sector initiatives supportive of sustainable farming practices, community-based farming, and farmland protection.

The following is an excerpt from a 2008 interview with Gary Gumz, who acted as MPIA director from 1998 to 2002:

Here in Madison County and surrounding areas we still had many family farms, but most of them depended on tobacco for their primary income. MPIA could see the handwriting on the wall: tobacco farming was on its way out. Yet we couldn't see any local organizations helping farm families prepare for the inevitable changes coming. So that became a big part of MPIA's work. The Listening Project enabled us to build local and state partnerships which would help farmers transition to more sustainable practices.

We listened with a deep and abiding respect for our farmers. Some of us had negative feelings about the health and environmental effects of tobacco and chemical farming. Yet we could also see that these forms of farming had provided a livelihood that enabled many small mountain family farms to keep going. We didn't judge or criticize farmers about growing tobacco or their use of chemical fertilizers and pesticides. We respected them and started with them right where they were. For example, sometimes tobacco farmers weren't ready to diversify into growing food crops. So we helped them see that growing organic tobacco was a way to increase their tobacco income. Then, once they had organic soil for tobacco, they would be able to gain organic certification, which would enable them, when ready, to transition into growing organic food or meat, which sells for more than non-organic products.

In other cases, some tobacco farmers were ready to diversify by moving from tobacco to food crops, but they were unsure about going organic. So we started by helping them transition into growing food crops and developing markets for their products. At the same time, we helped create educational opportunities for farmers to learn about the many benefits of organic growing. Whenever a farmer was interested and ready to go organic, we had programs that would help them learn effective organic growing practices, earn organic certification, and develop markets for their products.

What follows is the story of one Madison County farmer's transition from tobacco farming to diversified crops and organic

53

farming. That transition was not only an economic success - it also brought new vitality and health to family and community.

From Tobacco to Organic Food Production

~Narrative by Aubrey Raper

It was a snowy night in February. I almost decided not to go to what I had heard was an informal meeting of farmers, being organized by the Mountain Partners in Agriculture. This meeting was to be a discussion and listening time among farmers. It was to help us consider new markets and possibly new crops we might want to grow. I almost didn't go, but I did, and that little meeting changed our lives. We met at the Bantam Chef, where all of us farmers talked and listened to each other about what we took to be the issues facing us. We heard other farmers speaking about things they were producing that we weren't, and in fact, they talked at length about the vitality of their market and their crops. One in particular—Tom Elmore—became a really good friend of ours over the years. He really intrigued me with what he was producing and where he was marketing, and what the value of those crops were. That evening linked me to a new way of looking at our farming, and I saw in it a new opportunity. So what I took away from that first open meeting was the continuing sense that we could be doing something else with the farm. That's how it all began in 1995. My wife, Linda and I were tobacco farmers, and there were increasing problems with tobacco. We realized that we'd gotten too tied to tobacco, and the meeting made me aware of new possibilities that other farmers had already been successful with.

This first meeting was different from other meetings or workshops for farmers. For one thing, we weren't just being given information and being told what we should do. We were given some information about new market possibilities, but it was the discussion and listening among us farmers that really got us to thinking. When I left that meeting I knew it was time for me to start working my way out of tobacco farming.

So that meeting was in the wintertime. The next growing season Linda and I finished and marketed another tobacco crop. By that spring, we already were in the process of beginning to think of a different form of production and marketing. That summer and the following summer, we began the transition from being tobacco producers to growing lettuce and various greens, with some summer fruiting crops, squashes and different tomatoes.

Another listening event occurred later in the spring of '95 at AB Tech in Madison County. The group Linda and I were in was all farmers. Together we worked on our thoughts about farming. What came out of our group were three challenges: (1) Access to healthcare was a primary mover of farmers away from farming—trying to find work that had benefits. (2) To grow a diversity of crops, we needed a better selection of new things. (3) How to grow crops that had a positive market association. So those three things were always on farmers' radars. If we had good products and good markets, we could make enough income and be able to afford health care and stay in the farming business.

Tom Elmore was a primary guide for many of us. He was a farmer and worked with the Carolina Organic Growers (COG). Tom has the greatest commitment to farming of anyone I know. Tom and another farmer, John Roland, had already experimented with different varieties of organic crops that were good for transitioning into organic certification and sales.

The vitality that came out of all this discussion was incredible for both Linda and me, and of course, our kids benefited as well. We were really happy to be growing food and not tobacco. It was also exciting to be growing a diversity of crops. Part of the relationship with Tom was learning about an existing market—the organic market. So we were then transitional organic and we were welcomed into the Carolina Organic Growers (COG) marketing association. From our first formal meeting with that organization, we were able to be active participants and active marketers within that system.

Our relationship with MPIA continued to get stronger. In that first year and a half, MPIA turned into Appalachian Sustainable

Agriculture Project (ASAP), which later became its own organization. As we closed out the year of MPIA, we went down to Raleigh for a formal presentation of the project and I was a speaker. My story was that farmers were interested in sustainability and organic meat and crops because of our new successes. We had statistics of how our income had grown—doubled or even tripled. Also, our crop diversity had grown, our market had grown, and all of this happened in a relatively short period of time. Over three years, we'd transitioned to a whole new world of agriculture. What a fine time to be changing what you were doing!

I became a transition program coordinator with MPIA, which evolved into the Appalachian Sustainable Agriculture Project (ASAP), and I got some Kellogg Foundation funding. For three years I hosted well-attended field days for farmers on all kinds of things. I was trying to get farmers thinking outside the box that they had been farming in. The future of tobacco was really uncertain and farmers were beginning by 1998 to look for alternatives.

On most of those field days, tobacco growers were present. What did I see come out of that? I saw a real large tobacco farm in Haywood county transition to organic tomato and bell pepper production. A Madison County farmer transitioned from tobacco to hydroponic lettuce production. There's a long list of people who changed or broadened their operations.

One benefit of associating with COG was that there was such a diversity of crops among the 20 growers spread across NC—and, of course, we would get together twice a year, for a summer and a winter meeting, and we were learning from each other.

Sometimes learning from each other happened in unexpected ways, like when we invited the COG market manager, Mark Lewis, out to our farm for lunch. He came and brought his family. We were walking over a footbridge that crossed the spring that's the water source for our house. We had a beer in our hands, and as we sat on the footbridge, Mark saw watercress growing in the spring. Many years before, a friend of ours had given us some watercress and we had set it in the head of that spring. The spring very quickly became engulfed in watercress, which we used a little bit of in the house. But mostly we looked at it as invasive because it was covering up our spring.

So Mark Lewis said, "Why aren't you selling that?" I said I didn't know we could. "Yeah, we can," he replied. So we added watercress to our crop list and soon sales on it had just exploded. The interesting thing about that was we were still tobacco farmers when our spring was engulfed in watercress. On my way to the tobacco field I would cross the footbridge and I would look at the watercress overtaking the spring and remind myself that I needed to be getting the weed eater to clean it out from the spring bed. Then I'd walk on over the bridge to hoe the tobacco field. Within a year of that conversation on watercress with the market manager, we earned, in the first year of sales, more watercress dollars than we ever netted on tobacco production on three acres. It ain't rocket science to say that we'd been missing a real opportunity. A few years later we were out of tobacco production altogether, and watercress became our cornerstone crop.

Early on, COG had 20 growers statewide. When Linda and I joined, COG's gross sales were $75,000 statewide. The largest part of that was from a mushroom farmer in Yancey County. The next year, 1996, I was elected president of COG. Sales grew to $125,000 in 1996, and then gradually to $700,000 in consecutive years. That success signified to us there was a growing consumer interest in organic crops produced in North Carolina and such an enormous potential for growth in production and sales. The organization got large enough, and transportation and distribution costs were exorbitant, so in 2003 the eastern growers formed their own organization: ECO (Eastern Carolina Organic). Everything we produce stays here. Now and then a load of butternuts goes down east and a load of sweet potatoes comes back up. Sales today are really, really good.

I've spoken to many farmers about our farm's transition. I often go back to that snowy winter night when I almost didn't take the opportunity to listen and learn from other farmers. This transition has certainly been economically good for my family. It also brought a lot of vitality into our lives. It was good for our mental health. Now we're engaged in something new, exciting, and healthy for everyone.

Accomplishments of Mountain Partners in Agriculture

Interviews with individuals are at the heart of all projects but Aubrey's story is one example of the many diverse types of listening that can occur in different ways and places in the course of a project. Aubrey was not interviewed during the initial surveys, yet that first MPIA meeting changed his life, because farmers were able to share information, stories and ideas that led to concrete solutions.

What follows is an excerpt from a 2002 report outlining MPIA/ASAP accomplishments within one of the four MPIA priorities identified through their Listening Project:

Sustainable Production Systems:
- *Mountain Partners in Agriculture…provided financial, technical, and marketing support to 32 farming operations in the French Broad River basin of the mountains of Western North Carolina. This included the exceptional "Get Fresh- Buy Appalachian" campaign, which enlisted the support and participation of local restaurants, groceries, tailgate markets, and newspapers. ASAP also provided support to the agriculture education program at Madison High School and the Madison County Bee Keepers Association.*

- *The ASAP Transition Program demonstrated that sustainable and organic production is feasible and profitable and well-suited to the diversity of growing conditions in the mountains. This was done through: (1) farmer-to-farmer mentoring, (2) the experience and innovation of mountain growers, (3) the involvement of the local Cooperative Extension Service, (4) increased access to small financial grants, technical assistance and supportive networking.*

- *Twelve of the ASAP Transition Program participants, including eight burley tobacco growers, became certified for organic vegetable, organic burley tobacco, and organic apple production. They gained access to the expanding organic market through membership in Carolina Organic Growers, Inc.*

- *ASAP conducted six field days during 2000, with about 20 farmer participants at each field day. Three farm field days during 2001 focused on organic tomato, organic broccoli, and organic apple production and marketing, with over 100 area growers and extension agents attending.*

- *ASAP provided direct support for four demonstration farms for on-farm research and demonstration of sustainable practices.*

- *In cooperation with the Asheville-Buncombe Technical Community College, the NC Cooperative Extension Service, and Carolina Farm Stewardship Association, MPIA/ASAP developed the "Sustainable Mountain Farming Program", a series of courses and workshops for new and experienced farmers interested in sustainable agriculture, organic certification, and alternative production systems. The experience from this initiative helped develop appropriate sustainable farming programs at other community colleges in the region. These efforts were coordinated with local high school agriculture education programs and the USDA Natural Resource Conservation Service. Over 150 participants were served by the Sustainable Mountain Farming Program.*

Now, years later, ASAP has become a highly respected and influential force for sustainable agriculture in the entire western North Carolina region. For further information visit ASAP's website at http://www.asapconnections.org/.

Chapter 11

Building Pride, Resources, and Community-Based Change in Pleasant City

~Narrative by Tom Fischer

Pleasant City is the oldest black community in West Palm Beach, Florida. In 1994 and 1995, 106 residents of the area were interviewed by their neighbors, who had participated in a Listening Project training. It was organized by the United Sisters of Pleasant City, who decided that the best way to get their neighbors' energized into action was to go into their homes and listen to what they had to say about their concerns and suggestions for improvement.

Residents of lower-income areas are often left out of important decisions about their own neighborhoods. They are not asked to share their experience with what strategies have worked, failed, or are likely to succeed. The LP conducted in Pleasant City illustrates these issues well. This particular neighborhood had experienced many of the same challenges that other inner-city neighborhoods across the country face. A once-thriving corridor of locally-owned and operated businesses was now mostly boarded up. Manufacturing firms that previously provided jobs had relocated to "safer neighborhoods" or abroad in search of cheaper labor. Open-air drug dealing, violence, and crimes against people and property had become commonplace.

A West Palm Beach public official declared that local government wanted to "draw the line on crime" in several of the city's neighborhoods, including Pleasant City. Meetings took place, consultants from the public and private sector were called in, and important initiatives moved forward. All of this took place with little or no involvement from the people who had the most at stake in addressing those issues: the people who lived in that neighborhood.

It was announced that local government was going to buy the vacant elementary school in Pleasant City and convert it into a service center. A group of residents began to voice their concerns. The school in question had educated African-Americans in the area for many years before desegregation. That building held a very special place in the hearts of many in the community, especially the elderly who had attended the school. Residents asked questions such as, "Who will decide which programs should be provided at such a center?" and "Who will make decisions about renovation of this historic building?"

The United Sisters of Pleasant City were operating in the neighborhood as a loose-knit support group for each other at that time. They would welcome new moms into the neighborhood, advise them of available resources, help each other out with child care, and show women that they were not alone in the struggle to keep their children well and safe, pay the bills, and hold on to a belief that they had value and worth in the world.

This group stepped up and decided to conduct a Listening Project to make sure that resident voices were heard regarding this center and other neighborhood issues about which they cared deeply. The neighborhood interviews conducted as part of the LP also provided an opportunity to identify skills and assets of area residents that could be utilized and shared at a center. One woman said she would like to come in and talk about the career of nursing. A young man said he would love to conduct a class on building model cars. An elderly resident wanted to read to young children once a week. The LP helped create a feeling of ownership of the center among the residents.

Once the Pleasant City neighborhood interviews were completed, an all-day action-planning meeting was held, guided by a summary of resident responses from the LP. West Palm Beach city and county commissioners were there; the police chief was there; high-ranking aides to the mayor were there—but this meeting was different. Residents turned out in record numbers. They talked and the "experts" listened. The LP process helped identify and give legitimacy to the voice of residents who had previously been unheard or ignored.

The United Sisters became stronger and more visible, thus ensuring that residents had an ongoing voice and a hand in what happened to their neighborhood. When movement towards making the promised neighborhood center began to waiver, this group and its allies stood up to press for the center to become a reality. When the former black elementary school was eventually renovated and converted into the Pleasant City Multicultural Center, women from United Sisters were hired to provide support services to women, families, and children in the area. To this day, this Center remains a source of pride and self-determination in Pleasant City.

The LP process was not the primary reason that positive changes occurred in Pleasant City. These changes occurred because of the courage, tenacity, vision, and organizing ability of a small group of women. Their hard work, with the support of trusted allies, made the neighborhood center and other positive improvements a reality. The LP process did, however, provide a structure to help accomplish the following:

1. Give visibility to and ultimately help strengthen a resident leadership group.

2. Encourage the formation of a coalition of public and private organizations working with and supporting the resident leadership group.

3. Identify or "map" the strengths and assets of individuals living in a neighborhood so that they could be mobilized for neighborhood development efforts.

4. Focus the resident leadership group and its support network on identified, specific neighborhood development activities.

The United Sisters of Pleasant City: In Their Own Words

Below is the story of Corletta Clay's call to action. She is the president and founder of United Sisters of Pleasant City and the executive director of Kids Kompact.

Back in 1991, I remember spending a lot of time in James Grocery, a store owned by Paul Brown in Pleasant City. Paul was always encouraging me to get involved in neighborhood activities. One day, when the mayor of West Palm Beach was scheduled to come and speak in Pleasant City, Paul came knocking on my door. He wanted residents to get out and show the mayor that there were people who supported revitalization efforts in our neighborhood. After the speech I went up to talk to the mayor. I said that I hadn't heard anything about the needs of single mothers and their children and I thought that their needs were central to any successful revitalization in Pleasant City.

Afterwards, I went home and sat at my kitchen table, praying and thinking about what was and was not said at the meeting. I'm a preacher's daughter. I turn to prayer and my Bible to help find direction. It is this line from the Bible that later became the motto for the United Sisters of Pleasant City: 'Without a vision, my people will perish.'

Kids Kompact Mission Statement

The mission of Kids Kompact is to reclaim our community's faith and unity. Through the utilization of academic and cultural education, collective work, and cooperative economics, we can assist our families in regaining their traditional greatness. Kids Kompact accomplishes its mission by:

- *Working with families with young children, helping to make sure that*

63

they are ready for school and developmentally on target.

- *Working with pregnant women and teens, to ensure they are receiving the best prenatal and postnatal care possible.*
- *Identifying, working with, and providing referrals of core services for those who are considered at risk for substance abuse, domestic violence, low-weight births, etc.*
- *Educating and working with teens in the community on issues of family planning and sexual responsibility.*
- *Encouraging and assisting women and teens to pursue higher education and improve their job skills.*

With the help of a local community activist, John Stroman, I met with other single mothers in the neighborhood who were thinking and praying about the crucial issues affecting sisters in Pleasant City. We all had a different focus for our concerns, which included teen girls and teen moms, collaboration and unity in the black community, and single adult mothers. However, we shared the common vision of women supporting other women. We just started knocking on doors and talking to other single moms. We asked women about their pressing needs; we told them about resources that we were aware of; we helped set up a network of women helping each other with child care; and we helped organize baby showers for the new arrivals into Pleasant City.

Those days were the beginning of the United Sisters of Pleasant City. I'm very proud of what United Sisters has become and what we've accomplished. In August of 1994, United Sisters organized an all-women's conference called "Save Our Sisters." The conference brought together African-American women from a broad spectrum of economic and vocational backgrounds to address common concerns and work towards a more unified approach to addressing those issues. The Pleasant City Listening Project was a main focus of United Sisters. Also, United Sisters had an important role in shaping the Kids Kompact program (see sidebar) which works with the women and children of this neighborhood. In many ways, the prayers that I said at my kitchen table back in 1991 are being answered.

LaTanzia Jackson is also a member of United Sisters of Pleasant City and is the Family Service Coordinator for Kids Kompact. Below is her story:

When I moved into public housing in Pleasant City I had two kids, I was pregnant, and didn't have a job. The apartment was so cold in the winter that water and mildew formed on the walls. When I gave birth to twins, they both developed bronchitis. I felt so hopeless and cut off. I remember that I put up black blinds to keep the world out. My self-esteem was below zero.

A turning point in my life occurred when I noticed some women in my neighborhood who were beginning to reach out to other women. I saw women caring for each other, help each other out, and start talking about what they really wanted for their lives, their children, and their neighborhood. When Niema Kaid came to my door, she asked me questions and listened to me. That brought some of the hope and belief in myself that I had started to lose. Over time, I became very involved in helping to organize other women in Pleasant City. Through my involvement with United Sisters, the tenants' council, and Kids Kompact, I have come to realize that I have something important to contribute to others.

My daughter is an artist; she loves to draw. I remember that when we lived in public housing in Pleasant City she would want to go out on the back porch to sit and draw. I wouldn't let her go out, because I didn't want her view of the world shaped by the things that she might draw sitting out there, like winos drinking and fighting in the back yard. My daughter's pictures always seemed to have clouds in them. Back then, when my self-esteem was so low and I had so little faith in myself, I believed that she saw those clouds in me. I now know that I am not limited in any way. With the support and guidance of God, my family, my community, and the many strong women in my life, I know that I can do anything. My daughter's pictures are happier and brighter now. The clouds are gone.

Chapter 12

It Seemed to be a Losing Battle: Small Steps Lead to Big Change in Winchester

~ *Narrative by Geoff Huggins*

I sat at my desk, feeling discouraged and weary—and unable to get in touch with what was causing it. It was a troubling mood that had slowly been creeping up on me the last couple of weeks. I had just transcribed the notes from our most recent Listening Project interview. I'd added the information to the tally sheets that I was keeping. This was interview number 20 and counting.

Despite my downcast mood, the interviews had been going quite well. Residents of Winchester's North End neighborhood were welcoming the opportunity to talk about their feelings and concerns. Most had greeted our interview teams pleasantly. They had lots to say about how much they liked their neighborhood. But we were also hearing stories of the many stubborn problems. They told us that they were troubled by the drug sales, the run-down housing, trash strewn about, late-night noise, and poor relations with the police. It was a distraught neighborhood, although its residents still felt a strong attachment to it.

Some of the residents had joined our interview teams. That was a good sign that the process was gaining acceptance in the neighborhood, and that the community might indeed begin to organize to work for positive change. Despite these favorable signs, here I was: troubled by something I couldn't quite grab hold of.

I read through the responses again, revisiting scenes in my head of sitting in people's living rooms, listening to their replies to our questions. I began to recall hearing the same troubling concerns— over and over again. I remembered the frustration I heard folks express, as they recounted the times in the past that they'd tried to take action—only to encounter apathy in their own community or the deaf ears of city officials. I remembered empathizing with their sense of powerlessness as they watched drug sales occur out on the corner and wondered why the police couldn't seem to stop them. I remembered hearing the pride in their voices as they spoke of their deep-rooted and closely-connected community, in which they still felt safe, despite these problems.

As these memories came back, it began to dawn on me why I was so down. I was hearing the voices of people who were suffering from chronic, huge problems: drugs, poor housing, poor police relations, and bigotry. These troubles had slowly and uncontrollably been building for decades — even generations. They seemed by now to have become deeply embedded in the very fabric of the neighborhood. And this was not at all unique to my small town of Winchester, Virginia. Communities all across America were battling these same demons. Too often, it seemed to be a losing battle. I realized that I was starting to absorb their feelings of defeat and despair.

The Beginnings

I live in Winchester, a small town in the northern Shenandoah Valley of Virginia. It is a politically conservative city. Thus, while volunteerism flourishes here, activism in the social justice arena is not common.

I felt drawn to do something locally, but also felt cautious. Then one day in 1993, I discovered Rural Southern Voice for Peace (RSVP) through my Quaker contacts. This was an organization that seemed to fit me like a glove. It was rural—like my town. It was southern—I'd realized that organizing approaches being used in large northern cities often had a limited fit to southern regions. The folksy and pragmatic nature of RSVP's newsletter (Voices) inspired me. In its pages I read about activists who were taking action in their rural communities—dealing with similar issues to what I saw, and bringing change.

When first I read in Voices about RSVP's program called the Listening Project, I knew instantly that this tool was the one I wanted to use. It made good sense for my town, and for me. The concept of listening, as a basic approach to activism, appealed strongly to me. I was born a good listener. I had learned many times that listening had helped me to live a saner life than had talking. I sensed that, in order to identify a way to become effectively involved in my community (especially as a relative newcomer), I had to listen.

The Way Opens

My phone rang one spring morning. The woman calling said she'd heard that I knew how to do a Listening Project and wondered if I wanted her help to do one. She thought it would be a great way to launch a social justice project in our town. I stared at my phone, somewhat shocked at the coincidence, and at a loss for words. What had caused Katy to call me, just at the time I was seriously considering how to take the first steps towards exactly what she was proposing?

For the next several weeks Katy and I set about seeking an appropriate place where we might begin, and figuring out how to organize a team for our Listening Project. We met with one organization after another—describing the process to them and hoping they would come to agree that the Listening Project could be a powerful tool for them to use in their work.

One lead after another dried up, until our friend Don offered, "Hey, if you want to do something to bring positive change, how about coming to my neighborhood? We sure need it." He said, "The folks in my neighborhood don't want all these problems. They've tried for years to get someone downtown to listen to them and do something. If you want to try your project up there, I'll do everything I can to introduce you to people and get you started." Katy and I looked at each other, knowing without exchanging any words that we'd found what we were looking for.

Don lived in Winchester's North End community. The neighborhood had a negative reputation around town for being violence-prone and the center of the street drug trade. Many houses were in shabby condition. Some were empty and boarded up. The core population of the troubled neighborhood was predominantly black. Don was the city's first black councilor. He'd struggled to bring changes to his community, but his voice on city council was truly in the minority and often just politely listened to.

We began by forming a small team consisting of just the two of us and a couple of interested residents of the neighborhood. We spoke to a few community groups and visited churches—hoping to have more residents join us, and to form an organization to begin our Listening Project.

As Anglo-Americans, Katy and I faced some skepticism from the predominantly black population. We listened and talked, and listened some more. Gradually we built a very small team. Although we were almost too few to proceed with a Listening Project, we were highly dedicated. We decided that we would go ahead and plan our training, despite our small number; knowing that it meant some of us might be conducting many interviews. This would be a different approach from the typical Listening Project, where a larger team of volunteers is recruited by an established organization, well before interviews begin. Our plan was to start with our small crew and enlist additional team members as we went along—trying to organically grow an organization. It would require lots of enthusiasm and persistence.

My friend Rick Wilson came to Winchester to facilitate a Listening Project training for us. Our group developed a questionnaire, and Rick led our training on a wintry weekend. Slowly the interviews proceeded. We began by going to the families and friends of our team members. As the word spread in the neighborhood that we really were listening to them, more and more residents invited us into their homes. Soon, a few joined our ranks—including a young preacher from one of the neighborhood churches. Pastor John Guyton had been looking for a way to reach out to the wider community, to deal with some of the problems being faced by residents. He became a very powerful interviewer on our team. As a pastor, he naturally commanded respect in the community, and he was also blessed with the ability to listen deeply. The Listening Project process was rolling forward!

An Answer: Small Steps

But there I was, a few weeks later, looking over my compiled notes of the first twenty interviews—feeling as despondent as some of the more powerless residents we'd interviewed. It helped me a little, now that I understood what was bothering me: the overwhelming size of the problems. But I had no idea how to regain my confidence and move forward.

For the next few days I simply sat with my dilemma. Then a couple of days later, an answer came to me. First, I had to acknowledge that the struggle was both very large and extremely difficult. Yes, many of the problems being faced by the North End community were overwhelming. Yes, communities all over the country were facing similar struggles—and often losing. What community had fully succeeded in the "War on Drugs"? The whole country was losing this battle. Where had poverty and poor housing really been eradicated? Where had racial stereotyping been eliminated? These were stubborn problems that were not going to be resolved any time soon, and it wouldn't serve the interest of anyone in this community to build expectations that we could quickly make headway on them.

Insightful Comments on the Problems

- *"Do I feel safe? Yes, because we are surrounded by family and friends."*
- *"Drugs and trash – that's the problem. City officials just add to it, because they don't do anything until election time."*
- *"People judge us without knowing us. It doesn't feel good to live in a neighborhood that's classified as bad."*
- *"People see drug deals going down, but the police miss it. Police don't trust the residents' word. Their techniques don't work."*
- *"Some of these young people have no place to go – they live on the move. They've nothing to look forward to, no purpose in life."*
- *"I see the police in the daytime, when the drug men are sleeping. Where are the police at night?"*
- *"The city council treats the North End with disdain. They will*

70

be elected no matter what they do in the North End. There is no need to be answerable."

- *"Newspaper reporting is uneven. They don't investigate anything."*

Second, I began to notice that if I didn't allow my feelings to be swamped by those big problems, I found myself able to remember the creative and insightful comments that had been made by residents about many other smaller and more manageable problems they were also facing. That helped me to appreciate the imaginative ideas they had expressed about how they might face these concerns and bring positive change to their neighborhood. Those who lived in the community knew it best. The wisdom of a successful plan had already been expressed in the interviews. I wondered: How could these smaller ideas be acted upon, rather than have our efforts fail in trying to tackle the massive problems?

What hit me was that the task might be seen as manageable, if the priority was to begin by dealing with those smaller problems. No, the community could not expect to stop drug sales any time soon, or quickly end decades of apathy and feelings of disempowerment, or even quickly improve substandard housing. But residents could make some headway on a few of those smaller concerns they had identified. For example, many residents had described trash as an unsightly problem. Teams could be formed to pick up trash. Many others had cited the lack of communication between residents and police. Perhaps some form of dialogue between them could be started. Many of those interviewed had spoken of youth having too little supervision. A mentoring program might be started at the local elementary school; it would not only help the kids, but forge a closer connection between the community and the school.

Some Small Ideas for Change

- *"When the newspaper prints a story, tell them we need them to treat us with the same respect they do elsewhere."*
- *"Get the black churches united and working together, coordinating their activities."*
- *"We need children's programs – but they need to be in the neighborhood. Parents around here don't have*

transportation."

- *"Start a parental education program. Adopt a family, go out and work with families."*
- *"Form a citizen/police advisory committee. People could help them become more efficient."*

As my feelings of depression began to lift, I felt a renewed enthusiasm for the project. I realized that if the start-small approach was going to succeed, it would have to be adopted by the Listening Project team, as well as the community, as the way that made sense for them to proceed. As a facilitator, my job was to bring the Listening Project tool to the community and to assist them to organize and empower themselves—not to make decisions or do the work for them.

I presented the start-small approach to the group. They quickly decided to adopt it and began listing ideas for change that came out of the interviews, in the order of increasing difficulty. This process accomplished two important things. First, it helped the group to identify a relatively easy place to start. Folks could focus on that first small step and take action, quite confident of success. Second, the list created a step-by-step, ongoing game plan that laid out a path of progress. It was important not only to identify some starting point, but also to see the process as an ongoing one, so that they could build momentum that would begin with those early, small successes. As each step was taken, the community could look back, note the bit of progress made, gain a little more confidence, and tackle the next increasingly tougher step. It could bring a gradual process of empowerment.

Getting Started

The group did identify trash pickup as the first step. Even before interviews were completed, a small group of us met on a North End street corner one Saturday morning, with large trash bags in hand. Picking up trash is a highly visible job. As we filled bag after bag with debris and empty bottles, we stopped to chat with residents and let them know who we were. We talked about the

Listening Project interviews and the winds of change we felt stirring in the neighborhood. We invited curious kids to join us. Their natural enthusiasm lifted everybody.

That first step of trash pickup also provided the impetus for the group to decide they wanted to formally organize themselves as the North End Citizens. An organization of the same name had formed several years earlier, to create citizen patrols to face down the drug dealers in their neighborhood. They'd been energized by some initial success at that time, but had been unable to build enough momentum to keep it going. Since it was aimed solely at drug sales, group members soon became tired of street patrols. Without a broader agenda that included branching out to other activities, enthusiasm waned, the patrols stopped, and the group dissolved.

The re-forming of North End Citizens created an organization that both residents and city officials could see as an indicator of something happening. The young preacher, Jon Guyton, volunteered to chair the new group. North End Citizens began to hold its first meetings a few months before the Listening Project interviews were completed.

During those first few weeks of the formation of the North End Citizens, the process of building momentum was given a major boost by an unexpected decision of the Winchester Police Department to initiate a community-policing program. Across America, police officials were realizing that the current practice of responding to calls by radio-dispatched cruisers—while fast and efficient—had put distance between police officers and the residents they served. This gap had reduced communication and cooperation between police and citizens. Community policing is an effort to get back to a situation where residents and police officers know each other personally. In Winchester, the community-policing cops were being issued bicycles. They were instructed to ride through the neighborhood, meet residents, and get to understand the neighborhood better. We had their answer! The "bike cops" became the first city officials to get acquainted with the North End Citizens and to attend their meetings.

Over the next few months (starting in the summer of 1995), the North End Citizens took several more successful steps. Here is a list of highlights of some of their accomplishments over the first year or so:

- June 1995: First trash pickup.
- September 1995: Stimulated by the community-policing program, a cooperative relationship with the police department begins. Police come to know residents on a first-name basis, and begin to listen to what residents have to say about the drug trade and other safety concerns. In turn, residents begin to learn about the duties, abilities, and limitations of the police.
- September 1995: Two neighborhood parents and North End Citizens start an after-school activities and educational program for youth.
- October 1995: The North End Citizens begins to hold their meetings in the neighborhood's formerly all-black segregated school building, which had been closed for many years. The organization hatches a plan to lobby the city to rededicate the building as a community center. A coalition with other organizations is formed to achieve this goal.
- November 1995: The Listening Project is completed and a report is released. Presentations of the study's results are given around town. The local newspapers print several articles on the Listening Project results, as well as activities of the North End Citizens.

- March 1996: The North End Citizens establishes a connection with the neighborhood elementary school, helping to provide a cooperative relationship between the school and the Caretakers after-school educational programs. The interaction also leads later to a conflict resolution and nonviolence program at the school.
- June 1996: City officials, who have been attending North End Citizens meetings for several months, begin a constructive dialogue between residents and the city. In June, the Winchester

City Council awards the North End Citizens with a proclamation recognizing the organization for its accomplishments. The proclamation also pledges the council's ongoing support to the North End community.

- July 1996: The North End Citizens forms a housing committee—which begins to create a list of unsightly and unsafe properties in the neighborhood. The committee lobbies city officials to enforce its existing housing code, and to do something to improve the North End's substandard housing.
- January 1997: The city reevaluates its housing codes. Later, it updates them and begins to enforce them. The worst rundown rental properties begin to improve.
- March 1997: The city's school board responds to the requests to keep the previously segregated Frederick Douglas School open. It is rededicated as the Douglas Community Learning Center—providing a home for several of the city's educational programs, as well as dedicating permanent space for the Caretakers after-school program.

Listening Project Findings

This overlap of the Listening Project and the startup of the North End Citizens provided positive feedback for both of them. The Listening Project offered an organizing process for the North End Citizens. It brought out the voices of the community's residents and helped them find common ground, where they could come together and take action. In effect, the Listening Project provided the group with a game plan for action. In turn, the North End Citizens' activities and subsequent articles in the newspapers drew the attention of people all over the city. The word spread that something was happening in the North End and that something called a "Listening Project" had sparked the action.

By the time the interviews were completed and the Listening Project report was finished—some six months after the citizens' group began to form—residents in the North End and city officials wanted to hear what the report had to say. Our interviews showed that Winchester's North End neighborhood—although a troubled community in several ways—was also very stable. Its residents felt closely connected and rooted to their neighborhood. Signs were beginning to show that these close ties were unraveling, however, as the Winchester area rapidly grew and older residents in the neighborhood passed on.

Most respondents felt connected to their neighborhood and most of them felt safe, despite the problems. Half-way through the resident interviews (about the time that the North End Citizens began to form), we also began to interview a number of city officials. That allowed us to listen to their viewpoints about the North End, as well as give us an opportunity to inform them about what we were hearing from residents. By gathering the perceptions of both groups, we got a more balanced and broader perspective on the issues. This process also began laying the groundwork for a dialogue between officials and North End residents; in our interviews we shared with each group some of the things we had heard from their counterparts. Some seeds of communication were thus being planted, even as the interview process unfolded.

A Partnership is Formed

When the report was finished, the North End Citizens took the story of Listening Project to their neighborhood. Word spread informally in the close-knit community. The North End Citizens also held public meetings and gave presentations to various groups and organizations around town. Going outside their neighborhood with the results helped to disprove some of the stereotypes held by people in other parts of Winchester—that the North End residents were apathetic and uncaring about the poor conditions in their neighborhood. The city learned that although North End residents felt closely connected, they also felt disempowered and demoralized. Events were beginning to bring change, however. Residents were starting to feel enthusiastic and empowered. In turn, city officials greeted the news with enthusiasm. Many of them had wanted to see the situation in the North End improve, but lacked an understanding of where to start.

This is, in fact, one of the major messages of Winchester's North End Listening Project: In communities like this—where drugs, poverty, and other problems have taken hold—neither city officials nor residents want these things to happen. A lack of communication between the two groups, however, is a recipe for continued failure. Residents and city officials must find a way to cooperate with each other, if change is going to happen. The Listening Project in Winchester's North End helped bring residents and city officials together in a partnership that found ways to set aside previous conflict and mistrust and replace them with cooperation and mutual regard.

Over the ensuing eight years, progress steadily occurred in Winchester's North End community. The following list highlights some of the later accomplishments:

- North End Citizens (NEC) launches neighborhood survey to update and broaden the initial Listening Project findings.
- Winchester is awarded a federal grant to place resident police officers in the North End and to partially fund the Caretakers youth group. NEC forges an alliance with Habitat for Humanity, which plans to build several houses in the North End. Several city officials regularly attend NEC meetings, continuing the dialogue.
- A new Listening Project begins in Winchester's South End, where residents are concerned about substandard housing and misunderstandings with new Hispanic residents. (In the wake of this second Listening Project, a second citizen group is spawned, and the city begins to address improvements in rental housing in the South End. The city also establishes several types of city outreach programs to Hispanics.)
- The city hires a new housing code enforcement officer (filling a slot that had been vacant for years), who begins a close association with the NEC.
- February 1998: Winchester police urge passage of two new ordinances directed at controlling loud noise and public drinking—two often-cited concerns expressed during Listening Project interviews and actively lobbied for by the NEC.
- The nonviolence program at the elementary school expands. The students initiate a community service program to aid older

residents in the community.

- A second federal grant program provides for another resident police officer in the North End, as well as a resident officer in the South End.
- Eight new Habitat houses are planned in North End. The police and NEC partner to get additional street lights in the neighborhood.
- Habitat plans yet three more houses in the North End.
- The city's district attorney forms a Public Safety Committee to coordinate and plan city programs to improve the quality of life of residents. NEC and South End Citizens are invited to provide citizen representation.

The Legacy

After all these changes, we might ask, "What about all those big problems—drugs, poverty, poor housing, stereotyping—that had me and many North End residents depressed, years ago? Have they been eliminated yet?" No. Having had a long time to build, they will not disappear overnight. The struggle continues. There are still drug sales. Many houses still look run down or are boarded up. Apathy has not been uprooted. A lot of change has come to the North End, but there is still much to be done.

So how may we evaluate the success of the efforts of residents? One way is to make a long list of the specific accomplishments. But a very different measure of the effectiveness of the work is to describe how it has touched and transformed individual lives. I will close by describing how two lives were changed. Although no one knows how long the North End Citizens will continue to work for change, or how effective they might be, the positive impact of events on the lives of these two people is unmistakable.

1. The DCLC and Natasia

It was not until 1963 that Winchester began to integrate its public schools. In 1966, the Frederick Douglas School graduated its last all-black class. A few years later the building was closed. For years the old school sat empty and unused—but never vandalized. It seems that residents had a fondness for the building that prevented its mistreatment. Since it was right in the center of the North End neighborhood, those of us involved in the Listening Project received permission to hold some of our meetings there. This started a process towards reclaiming the old Douglas School as a community center—that none of us could have foreseen.

After the North End Citizens formed, an early consensus developed among its members that the venerable old school should never close again. The group allied itself with the Douglas School Alumni Association and other groups. They signed up several community organizations that would be interested in using the old school, and began lobbying the school department to transform the building into a community center. They found a receptive ear in the superintendent of schools.

A year later the Douglas Community Learning Center (referred to as the DCLC) was dedicated. It now houses a number of neighborhood community groups, as well as several school special-education programs. The youth group Caretakers (which had been started about that time by a couple of neighborhood moms) was given permanent space in the building to hold its after-school programs.

Natasia began attending the Caretakers programs when she was in sixth grade. By going to the DCLC each afternoon, she found herself in a healthy environment. Natasia's dad was in jail for drug sales. Her mom worked long hours, which cast many responsibilities on Natasia's shoulders. Caring for her three younger siblings often kept her from her schoolwork.

Natasia's grades had been very low. Her self-confidence was equally low. She enrolled in the Caretakers' tutoring program, to get the special attention that might bring her success at school. Her tutor wondered why she did not show up some afternoons—not realizing that Natasia was sometimes prevented from being there by yet another family crisis. It was not a lack of motivation that kept her back—it was the load of responsibilities in a family dealing with serious problems. But Natasia persisted. The organizers of Caretakers knew well the struggles its kids were dealing with, and had the understanding and determination to give them lots of support.

Natasia very slowly gained confidence. Her grades gradually went from abysmal to good. She became a leading member of Caretakers step-dance team—giving her and the other girls on the team a major boost in self-confidence. She graduated from high school—not becoming a dropout, as many had expected. In fact, Natasia earned a scholarship to a private college.

2. Housing: Mary's Passion

Mary began attending some of the early meetings of the North End Citizens. She was very quiet at first—she just watched as others spoke about their concerns.

Mary's interest—her passion—was the poor housing conditions in the community. She was disturbed by the many rundown and trashy houses. She knew that most people in her neighborhood rented and she had learned that many landlords appeared to care little about how dilapidated their rental properties were. She also knew that tenants were not appropriately screened and often abused their apartments. She wondered why it was that other parts of town looked much neater. Mary took pride in her home and didn't understand why others didn't feel the same.

Mary quickly found a few other folks at the meetings who were also interested in raising the quality and safety of housing in the neighborhood. They formed a housing committee within the North End Citizens, and began to meet on their own. Mary would corner some of the city officials who had begun attending North End Citizens meetings and press them with questions. She learned that the city did indeed have a housing code that was intended to prevent or fix the kinds of problems that bothered Mary—such as broken windows, fallen gutters, inoperable cars and appliances discarded in the yard, trash strewn around, and overgrown shrubs that hadn't seen a pruning for many years. Yes, the city did have a housing code, but it became obvious to Mary that the city housing inspectors rarely came into her neighborhood.

As she probed and learned more, Mary and the housing committee developed a plan to document the problems. The committee made a long list of properties that needed attention. They took photos. They went to the city's housing official. They woke the city up to the magnitude of the problems, and more importantly, delivered the message that North End residents were no longer going to be passive about their rundown housing.

As Mary dug a little deeper, she learned even more. She found out that the city already had the legal means to bring improvement. Not only did the city have a housing code, it had a position called "Code Enforcement Officer," a person who could demand those improvements. She was amazed to find out that this position had been vacant for several years!

Mary and the committee invited the city's planning and zoning directors to a North End Citizens meeting. In the public limelight, the officials promised action. They formed a working group of residents and landlords, which reviewed the situation and made several recommendations about how the city could get proactive. The city council advertised to fill the vacant position of code enforcement officer.

A few months later, Winchester's new housing officer, Ms. Angelia Alford, arrived. Mary and Angelia worked closely together. They began gently but insistently informing landlords— with written notice and accompanying photos—that their properties must be cleaned up and made safer. The Housing Committee formed a repair team to help poor and elderly homeowners make repairs. As Ms. Alford had pointed out, "If an elderly widow who owns her home gets cited for a broken rain gutter, why penalize her? Wouldn't it make more sense to give her a hand to fix the problem?" The repair team got local merchants to donate supplies and fixed up several neighborhood homes.

About that time, a group of folks elsewhere in Winchester were forming the first local chapter of Habitat for Humanity. They knew that something was stirring in the North End, and wanted to pick up on the changes going on there. The president of Habitat came to a North End Citizens meeting and described Habitat's hopes for building some new homes in the community. Mary saw yet another opportunity and got involved. A vacant lot in the neighborhood was donated, and many folks pitched in to build Winchester's first Habitat home. The success of this enterprise spawned plans to build more houses.

Mary then became involved in the Habitat selection process—helping to identify North End residents who could qualify for these low-cost homes. Mary helped steer several residents through the application process.

Mary later filled a seat on Habitat's board of directors. Over the next few years some 19 new Habitat homes were built in the North End community. Today one can drive down what was once the most notorious street in the city and no longer be assailed primarily by the sight of many vacant and boarded-up houses and abandoned cars. There still are a few boarded up houses, but one's eye is now drawn to a neat row of tidy new houses, whose residents enjoy living in a home that they never would have believed they could actually own.

Chapter 13

Racial Justice in Keysville, Georgia

~ Narrative by Herb Walters

One of our earliest Listening Projects on race relations and community development was the Keysville Listening Project. Keysville is a small community about an hour from where I grew up near Augusta, Georgia. It has a majority African-American population and whenever I look back to my time in Keysville, I am inspired and grateful for all that they taught me.

In 1983, a small group of brave and committed African-American citizens in Keysville formed the Keysville Concerned Citizens. Their focus was on the serious problems facing their community. Seventy percent of town residents had no running water—they had to haul water every day to their homes. There was no sewage system, no street lights, health care facilities, or jobs. Illiteracy was a problem. During this process they learned that Keysville had been registered as a town and had been incorporated since 1890. This was upsetting news, because there had never been any municipal elections. Forming a local government could have provided a tax base for addressing some of the serious community needs and problems.

Keysville Concerned Citizens soon set the wheels in motion to hold elections, so they could vote for a mayor and town council that would begin addressing community needs. However, Keysville residents were split along racial lines over the issue. Representing a majority of the Keysville population, black residents saw an opportunity to elect officials who would address some of the serious issues facing the town. White residents, however, saw no need for change. Black residents felt that whites simply didn't want to have black elected officials. Statements made by some white residents seemed to support that feeling. The divide grew.

A series of legal struggles ensued, with some white residents successfully challenging election results. The legal struggles and the involvement of Southern Christian Leadership Conference and the Christic Institute brought the struggle to the nation's attention, with TV vehicles and national news reporters, including Time and Newsweek, flocking to the town. Keysville was soon being seen as a clear example of racism that would not allow black residents to elect a government that could benefit the community. White residents resented the outside intruders, and the racial divide seemed to deepen. In the end, the elections were deemed legal, and Keysville elected a town council that had only one white member, led by a dynamic black Mayor: Mrs. Emma Gresham.

A short time later, Mayor Gresham invited RSVP to conduct a Listening Project in Keysville. Despite the adamant opposition to the new government from some white residents and no cooperation from others, Mayor Gresham remained committed to creating a town that respected and served all its residents. She saw a Listening Project as a way to reach out to white residents and gain their support for the new government's efforts for community improvement. For interviewers, RSVP paired up non-resident whites with resident African-Americans. Thus, bi-racial teams of trained listeners began interviewing white residents. Interviewers asked questions which demonstrated that the new city council and mayor really wanted to hear their concerns and their ideas for community improvement.

Given the history of the situation, this was another case where interview teams went out with considerable apprehension. Once again, however, they returned relieved and happy with what they found. Ideas for improvement were put forward, and some white residents were supportive of some of the changes that could come, now that Keysville had a city government. When asked if they were willing to try to improve race relations in the community, a significant number of interviewees were willing. It was also learned that for some of the white residents, a primary reason for their opposition to the city government was based on their fear of increased taxes on an already minimal income.

There were, of course, some white residents who remained adamantly negative about the new city government and its black leadership. Negative racial beliefs and attitudes had existed in Keysville for many years, going back to times of slavery. So while the Listening Project brought a breakthrough, it certainly did not end the ongoing struggle to overcome racial prejudices and conflict. However, it did provide some hope, and it provided an opportunity for some white residents, who previously would have nothing to do with the new town government, to offer their ideas for community improvement and to voice their approval of the work that the new city government was embarking on. It revealed that it was not simply a black-versus-white issue—and described some ways to move forward. In fact, Mayor Gresham reported to Listening Project RSVP that she was able to secure support for their efforts from a previously unhelpful state official after she showed him the results of the Keysville Listening Project. These results assured the official that Keysville cared about all its citizens, black and white.

A second Listening Project in Keysville continued getting citizen input into city progress. Mayor Emma Gresham noted in an Atlanta Journal article, "…the Listening Project played a positive role in opening communication and helping us understand each other and how to work together." The primary reason for progress in Keysville, however, is the dedicated work of Keysville's citizens, including Mayor Gresham, the Keysville City Council, and the Keysville Concerned Citizens.

Chapter 14

I Don't Trust Muslims Any More

~ Narrative by Herb Walters

It is 1992. The nightmare of ethnic cleansing is a reality for thousands of Serbs, Croatians, and Muslims in the former Yugoslavia. There is repeated news of mass killings, neighbors turning on neighbors, the horrors of concentration camps, and the destruction of entire ethnic communities. I have been asked by the European Civic Center for Conflict Resolution to go to Serbia and offer Listening Project training to a group that is trying to bring some sanity to the chaos.

I reach my destination by flying to Hungary, then traveling by train into Serbia, where I meet my contact, Stevo. He tells me that the initial proposal for a Listening Project is no longer possible, since he and others have had to go underground to avoid trouble with the Serbian authorities. Instead, I am sent on to the city of Pancevo (which is located a dozen miles east of Belgrade, the capital of Serbia). There I am to discuss with members of a local group, the Pancevo Peace Movement (PPM), the possibility of conducting a Listening Project in Brestovac, a village of about 3,000 Serbs and 300 Muslims. On my way to Pancevo, I am sobered by Stevo's final warning to me: "If the U.S. acts on its threats to take military action against Serbia, you could be arrested by the Serbs as an American spy."

When I arrive in Pancevo, I am told that ethnic tensions in Brestovac are very high. Weeks earlier, a fight between a Serb and Muslim on a bus led to an attack on another young Muslim. Serbs chased the Muslim, shouting, "We will drink your blood." Two days later I am told of two other incidents in the village: A Muslim woman was heard shouting ethnic slurs at a Serb, and a 12-year-old Muslim boy was badly beaten by a young Serb. There are
86

rumors that both Serbs and Muslims are stockpiling arms. Fear—
the first prerequisite to ethnic cleansing—is taking hold in
Brestovac.

The members of PPM and I meet with the village leaders of
Brestovac to see if they will approve the use of a Listening Project
and the involvement of PPM in their community. They are
determined to put a stop to the downward drift into violence and
cautiously accept PPM's proposal to conduct a Listening Project.
They are convinced that there is a need for communication, that it
can help decrease some of the rumors and fears that are leading
people toward hatred and violence. We make plans to move
forward with a Listening Project.

That night, back in Pancevo, I stay in the small apartment of
Sladjina, a Serb. A round-faced, gentle woman in her 40s, she is a
single mother who deplores the killing and the hatred. As is true of
other members of PPM, Sladjina was not very political before the
war—but events have propelled her into action. Although there are
other Serbs who feel as she does, not many are as brave as Sladjina
and her fellow PPM members, who speak out and have taken
action for peace. Their bravery is undeniable, given that they
continually receive threats from Serbian patriots, who think that
anyone working for peace is a liar and a traitor to Serbia.

After a week of Listening Project planning and training, a dozen
teams of two listeners each go door to door throughout Brestovac
to conduct in-depth interviews with both Muslims and Serbs. The
purpose of these interviews is to open communication, build trust,
and find possible community-based solutions to the growing ethnic
tensions. Despite long hours of preparation and training,
interviewers are nervous and frightened, as they will be going into
people's homes and raising issues that have been the source of so
much death and destruction.

I accompany a listening team with an interpreter who helps
translate what is said into English. Our beginning questions are
easy openers, such as, "What do you like most about living here in
Brestovac?" Other questions, such as, "How is the present
economy affecting you?", and "What do you know about recent

fights between Serbs and Muslims?" slowly open discussion about problem areas and help us understand people's perceptions and feelings. With a foundation of trust established by respectful, honest listening, we can eventually ask questions such as, "Is there something about the Muslim or Serb people that concerns you?" and, "Why do you think that sometimes people focus more on differences than on their similarities?" Our interviews culminate with an emphasis on bringing forth positive ideas and solutions. We ask, "What do you think could be done to increase trust between the different ethnic groups here in Brestovac?"

The second interview I accompany is with an angry 17-year-old Serb, Mihovil, who is living with his parents. At first he seems open to our presence, but as we move into questions related to ethnic conflict, he begins to tense up and withdraw. He makes occasional hostile, angry comments about Muslims. "I hate Muslims," he says as he drops his head and looks down at the floor.

We continue, however, to treat Mihovil with respect, allowing his parents to interject statements when he does not answer our questions.

The interview begins to reveal many things. Mihovil's working-class family is suffering greatly from the war. The father has lost his job in a devastated Serbian economy. Every night the family watches Serbian broadcasts of Muslims killing Serbs. There is nothing for the youth or the unemployed to do anymore but sit around and talk about the killing, their anger, and their fear.

One of our questions asks Mihovil to speak about any Muslim friends he had in the past. He recalls that before the war everyone got along, saying, "We really didn't even know who was Serb and who was Muslim." He speaks with some emotion about his former Muslim friends.

"But all that is over now," he says. "Now I wish they would all go away from here. I don't trust any of them anymore. Nothing could ever be the way it used to be."

During the first half hour of the interview, we seem to be going nowhere with Mihovil. His body remains tense, his arms are folded, his face rigid and his hands sometimes clench into fists. His anger and hostility seem unshakable. I can tell that our interviewer is a bit concerned, and I think she is probably wondering if she's made a mistake to knock on this door.

We continue, however, to listen with empathy and compassion. The interviewer asks sensitive but thought-provoking questions. In the second half of the interview, Mihovil gradually begins to open a little and take interest. He is beginning to understand that he can say what he really feels—that we're not there to judge him or tell him what he should think. A crack in his armor appears when he tells us about the terrible conditions he and his unemployed family must now live in because of the war.

"It's terrible," he says. "My father hasn't had work for some time now, and it is hard sometimes to even have enough food. My parents worry so much. This war has changed everything. We have no youth center anymore and we no longer trust the Muslims who used to be our friends. When I watch TV, I see other Serbs suffering as well—being killed by Muslims."

The interview continues. Finally, there comes that dynamic moment when a person, knowing he is really being heard and understood, drops his fear and anger for an instant and goes deep into the center of his being.

"You and your family have suffered a great deal from this war," our interviewer says. "It seems like everybody is suffering on all sides: jobs lost, friendships and homes destroyed, and much death. Do you think there is anything that can be done to rebuild the trust and friendships that existed here before the war—so that you, your family, and all the people in Brestovac can return to a better life?"

Mihovil takes a deep breath and responds, "I think it would be good if we could reopen the youth center." We thank Mihovil for his response and ask him to explain. "The youth center was a place where young people of different ethnicities could get together in a friendly atmosphere. But the center was converted into a private restaurant, and now we have no place to do this. Instead, we remain separated and say bad things about the other side. Our fears and anger build because of all that we hear in the news and all the hardships in the village."

We tell Mihovil his idea is an excellent one that really could make a difference. We tell him that we believe in the ability of people like him and his family to make a better life for themselves and their community. For the first time, there is a very small smile Mihovil's face. He has moved from fear to hope. It is obvious that he appreciates our affirmation.

"Perhaps," he says, in response to our next question regarding action he could take, "I could participate in programs to bring peace back to our village." When we leave Mihovil's home, we promise that we will share his ideas with the village leaders who are also seeking peace. The whole family thanks us for coming and asks us to stay longer, but it is time to move on to other interviews. When all the interviews are completed and listeners gather to share their experiences, we find that other teams have also had difficult but positive experiences. The art of listening has been a healing process for us all.

After returning to my home in North Carolina, I learn that Mihovil's suggestion has helped influence community leaders in Brestovac to develop a youth program that helped open a door to inter-ethnic understanding.

Chapter 15

Bridging the Class Divide: The Piedmont Peace Project

~ *Narrative by Herb Walters*

Another of the early Listening Projects—conducted by the Piedmont Peace Project in North Carolina—helped establish the clear connection between peace and justice issues. In the 1980's PPP was one of the most effective citizen's organizations in the state. Why? Because they had some dynamite organizers, led by Linda Stout. Also, the members, who were mostly low-income or working-class people, were strongly affected by the high levels of U.S. tax dollars that went to military spending rather than human needs. Rather than detailing the danger of a possible nuclear war, they focused on the already existing dangers of citizens struggling and suffering from misguided economic priorities. And rather than calling in experts to point out the problem and offer their solutions, the PPP went directly to the homes of people who, like them, were caught in those struggles—including many African-Americans who were often ignored by the peace organizations.

PPP utilized their Listening Project to identify possible solutions. They enabled people normally not heard to consider and reflect on the imbalance between military and human-needs spending and how that impacted their lives. By listening to the people, PPP was also able to develop more effective educational material. Unlike much of the peace material written at that time—full of detailed information and statistics—PPP's material was simple, direct, and accessible to people with very low reading levels, a reality in many low-income communities.

Linda Stout, who founded this organization, recalls, "At Piedmont Peace Project, we were able to effect change in many areas by linking our issues and building a powerful force in our communities to be reckoned with. We educated and got out the vote of 44,000 people in our congressional district. We also mobilized people to lobby on issues that affected us."

In her excellent book Bridging the Class Divide, Linda recalls PPP's effectiveness on both justice and peace issues:

When we started PPP, our Congressman, Bill Hefner, had a zero percent voting record on peace issues and only about a 30 percent voting record on social justice issues. We lobbied him from the very beginning on the issues we were concerned about—housing, health care, child care, and education—and we talked to him about the military budget. For instance, in 1985 we lobbied against severe cuts that some were recommending to social security, disability, and health care funds. We organized four different groups to visit Congressman Hefner, all on the same day.

Linda writes that the first group was the peace group which advocated cutting funds for the MX missile, rather than cutting disability, social security, and other funds. She continues:

Then a group of low-income white folks we had worked with— mostly farmers—went to Hefner's office to talk about issues they were concerned about, including social security, farm subsidies, and the military budget. They also recommended cutting funds for the MX missile. The third group... was an African-American group. They talked about housing, health care, and educational opportunities for the youth and concluded by saying, 'We don't want you to vote for the MX missile. Use the money to invest in our communities.' Finally, in came a group of disabled folks who wanted to talk to Hefner specifically about cuts in the social security disability program.

When the fourth group called for cutting MX missile funds, Hefner just put his head down on the table in disbelief. Hefner, who had supported the MX missile, ended up voting against it. With repeated influence from PPP, his voting record moved to as high as 83 percent on peace issues and 98 percent on social justice issues!

Chapter 16

The Asheville Religion and Diversity Project

*The following account was excerpted from articles from the early 1990's, published in RSVP's journal, **Voices***

~ Narrative by Lynda McDaniels and Catherine Rogers

Gary Lukowicz still shudders when he recalls the hatred he encountered one day in 1992. He and other members of the Asheville Friends (Quaker) Meeting in North Carolina signed a public document in support of an event for the gay community. A rush of hate calls and letters followed; they threatened to boycott businesses, call employers, and put members of the Asheville Meeting on a "hit list."

This was, in fact, not an exceptional occurrence. A study by the Southern Appalachian Lesbian and Gay Alliance found that roughly half of their members had been victims of some form of hate activity. Many lesbians and gays, working in all walks of life, had to keep their sexual orientation secret for fear of discrimination that they would receive on the job, in finding housing, and other areas of their lives. Many had felt rejected, misjudged, or even hated by people of faith.

Says Lukowicz:

When I got the first call, my initial reaction was disbelief. We got some pretty nasty calls, including a threat to boycott my business. I got angry, but I soon realized my anger wasn't going to change things. Later on, my feelings changed to a deep sorrow, knowing that people seem to have to feel this way and show this much hate. I realized this is what it feels like to experience prejudice as an African American, Hispanic, gay, or lesbian. My experience was just a hint of what they must go through.

The Asheville Meeting decided to conduct a Listening Project to open communication with area religious leaders on the issue of homosexuality. To do so, they joined with others who supported their efforts to form the Asheville Religion and Diversity Project (RDP). What started as a short-term effort—trying to better understand feelings and fears—turned into a two-year project that resulted in direct communication and increased understanding between gays, lesbians, and many area religious leaders. It also led to an organization of religious leaders supporting religious, civil, and human rights for all people, regardless of race, ethnicity, culture, gender, sexual orientation, or creed.

RDP's first effort involved interviewing 50 religious leaders from the Asheville area who were mostly selected at random. Effort was also made, however, to visit with clergy who were known to have strong negative views about homosexuality. It was especially important that these voices be included. Interviewers were understandably nervous about interviewing religious leaders on such a divisive and explosive issue as homosexuality. Many had had the experience of reading about or hearing of ministers who condemned homosexuality, using words like "evil" or "abomination."

Interview Results

RDP interviewers did, in fact, encounter clergy who held firm with their condemnation of homosexuality and rejection of gays and lesbians. However, far more often they found clergy confused, or open to and interested in examining their feelings and faith in relation to homosexuality. One volunteer listener, Dawn, said:

"It seemed like ministers are a lot less hostile toward homosexuals than I thought they'd be. Even if they thought it was a sin, they weren't hostile." Another volunteer, Greg, said, "I expected ministers to be much more negative than they've been. I was surprised that the views I've heard are often beyond tolerance—more toward acceptance. I never expected to find such a large group that was somewhat confused about it all and interested in exploring their feelings about homosexuality. All the ministers I've talked to are interested in knowing about whatever RDP does as follow-up to our interviews."

Evaluation of RDP's Listening Project interviews yielded the following results:

- Nearly half of the interviewees did have some concerns and fears about homosexuality.
- One-quarter said that they could accept the person but not what they considered was the sin.
- Virtually all agreed that hate crimes and violence against homosexuals are wrong.
- Three-quarters of those interviewed felt that homosexuals should have equal civil rights.
- Over half felt that the church should accept homosexuals.
- Over half advocated tolerance, love, and acceptance.
- Two-thirds responded positively about homosexuals whom they knew.
- Over half did not think that gay people threatened the family.
- In most cases, those who thought homosexuality was a choice had more negative feelings about it, while those who thought it was likely inherited were more open or accepting.

One minister said: "The questions helped me formulate, in religious terms, what my feelings were on this issue. It was a small catalyst that helped me move forward in promoting tolerance and understanding." This minister started a very effective AIDS ministry based in his own church. After his interview, he decided to speak on a public radio show about his views.

According to RDP coordinator Sally Broughton, releasing the survey results to the media was an important part of the effort to counter public stereotypes of homosexuality. She said: "The survey helped us break our own stereotypes of the religious community. Some of us went into this project thinking that most of the religious leaders would be negative on this issue. The results taught us something as well."

Eddie Morgan, a southern Baptist minister, says, "It was an opportunity to let folks within the community knows that not every church, particularly not every Baptist church, thinks like the stereotype."

RDP interviews took place for a full year. Even before they were completed, certain patterns of response became clear. One such pattern was that, while many ministers were more open minded than expected, very few were doing anything to increase communication and understanding about homosexuality, or to be more actively inclusive of gays and lesbians. The reasons for this varied, but in many cases it was based on fear of alienating parishioners and on lack of knowledge of how gay and lesbian people suffered from discrimination and hate. Based on these patterns, the Religion and Diversity Project developed a task force that began planning what should be done when all interviews were completed.

A gay minister who wishes to remain anonymous, said:

I got involved because I wanted to work with ministers who might feel there is something inferior about homosexuals. I have a lot of concern and compassion for ministers in this situation. I believe that the churches have a long way to go in dealing openly and fairly with homosexuality. There is the question of whether people are born homosexual or whether it is a chosen lifestyle. If it is orientation (biological), and if, as we are increasingly discovering, this orientation is built in even before birth, then we have the question, "Does God make junk? The fact is, we are all God's children and this is not about choices. Why would anyone want to choose something that brings them so much hatred?"

Facilitated Group Listening

When LP interviews were completed, the task force began implementing their follow-up strategies. Those ministers who expressed an open mind, or were confused, or had "on-the-fence" feelings about homosexuality, were interviewed a second time. This second interview was shorter. It acknowledged their feelings

96

and provided the religious leaders with resources and opportunities that could help them continue to explore their beliefs and their response in relation to homosexuality. One of the questions in this second round of interviews asked them if they would be interested in small-group Group Listening with gay and lesbian people and other religious leaders.

A significant number of ministers expressed interest in listening and dialogue, and in receiving resources related to faith and homosexuality. RDP then responded to each request and organized several sessions of Facilitated Group Listening between religious leaders and homosexuals. RDP decided to use RSVP's new program: Facilitated Group Listening. Facilitated Group Listening (FGL) does not advocate a position; rather, it allows all sides to be heard. In the Religion and Diversity Project several listening sessions were conducted with small groups, each consisting of two gay or lesbian participants (or family) and two religious leaders. Each listening group was assigned an experienced, trained facilitator, and all participants agreed to a contract, under which they would consent to listen to others and be listened to, in a spirit of mutual respect and tolerance. There was no pre-determined outcome—only the desire to increase understanding.

This session made a strong impression on Reverend Bob Roach of the Biltmore United Methodist Church:

It was an eye-opening and heart-warming experience, because there was openness from both sides. Any time we can build bridges, it benefits the community as a whole. I think it helped me understand the discrimination these folks have experienced.

Participants shared their religious beliefs, experiences with prejudice, feelings about churches excluding homosexuals, and their ideas for positive change. Through the simple (yet difficult) act of listening, prejudices on both sides were able to be heard and allowed to unravel.

A participant in the listening session said:

I was in a group with a gay male and two Baptist ministers. During the process of answering questions that evening, one of the ministers came around 180 degrees. He had never talked to a gay person before, and that pointed out to me that a lot of the problem is with people who don't really know much about homosexuality; people who are dealing with feelings that came perhaps from their grandfather or grandmother. It was impressive for me to see someone who had never spoken with a gay person change his opinion when he was able to hear someone speak of their personal experiences. I am a member of Parents and Family of Lesbians and Gays (PFLAG), having a lesbian daughter. I have to remain confidential, however, because I cannot afford to lose my job.

Another participant, a carpenter living in a small town east of Asheville, appreciated the opportunity to speak directly:

Most of what we hear in the media portrays churches as being opposed to the lesbian and gay community. My feeling all along was that this probably wasn't a true picture. In the listening sessions, ministers had a chance to see those of us in the gay and lesbian community as real people, not just stereotypes. Maybe the next time they think about gay folks, they will have a different face to think about, maybe one that is more positive.

When the larger group reconvened to share their small group experiences, Chuck Taylor, a priest at St. John's Episcopal Church, was moved by what he heard:

It was just unbelievable—the emotional content of that gathering, the prayer in a circle at the end, the gays and lesbians who have experienced tremendous problems all their lives with a religious structure that represents society in so many ways. The pain on their faces made an impact on me; specifically to realize the depth of the pain that churches inflict on people.

One Asheville minister recalled:

It was quite an experience to hear from someone who works and contributes as a good citizen to this society, yet they must experience fear in every part of their lives—the fear of letting others know who they truly are. Fear of discrimination, rejection, and hatred, which could come at them from any direction—even the churches that profess the magnificent love of Christ. It was hard to hear of the hatred one man in our group has experienced, though he is clear that he was born the way he is and wants only to live a normal life.

The Religion and Diversity Project's follow-up to the Facilitated Group Listening included the goal of helping ministers turn their good will into positive action for education and change within their churches. Therefore, after each session, ministers were asked to commit to one action they could take to bring this issue out into the open. One participant recalls:

One Southern Baptist minister was so compelled by what he heard, he said to me, "I am going to write a sermon on this." And he did. He preached a very beautiful sermon the following Sunday.

Other ministers initiated outreach efforts that would be more inclusive of gays and lesbians in their church worship and programs, while some took steps to educate parishioners about issues of homosexuality and diversity. Lukowicz recalls:

There was a real sense of excitement and electricity in the air at this first gathering. Now there is a strong voice coming from the religious community, one that speaks out for diversity, equality, and justice.

One lesbian participant believes that the Religion and Diversity Project brought hope to a place where fear and confusion had reigned:

It's so strange that religious groups can preach love and understanding at one time and then preach sermons that cause people to fear, reject, or even hate human beings because they are different from them.

A participant, Megan Kaiser, recalls:

It was exciting to be able to address issues of homophobia in the churches.... The civil rights movement for people of color gained great momentum through the churches. For a long time, gays and lesbians have thought of the religious community as a source of rejection, hatred, and hypocrisy. Now that is changing.

The Interfaith Fellow for Justice

One long-term goal for the R&D Project was to have churches take more leadership on the issue of diversity. That goal, organizers feel, was met and solidified when several religious leaders who had been interviewed formed the Interfaith Fellowship for Justice. Their first meeting brought together about 50 religious leaders from Western North Carolina to develop programs on local and national justice issues.

Henry Hanson, of the Asheville Area Religious Network for Gay and Lesbian Equality, became a participant in the Fellowship. He recalls:

It can be devastating to people to be excluded from participating in the worship of God in the church of their choice, simply because they are who they are. The personal experience of knowing a gay man or a lesbian makes people more open on the subject; more interested in getting involved with solutions to the divisions and antagonism of the past. Many religious leaders feel that it is a risky thing to deal with, and it is. But now, through the Religion and Diversity Project, we've broken through some of the walls of separation and fear.

Project organizers admit there is still confusion and hostility in the churches about homosexuality, but the progress made is encouraging. What started off with hate calls seems to have ignited a new level of healing in Asheville and beyond. A similar project in another area of North Carolina, as well as projects in Atlanta, Portland, and Chicago were modeled on the Asheville Religion and Diversity Project.

Chapter 17

Grassroots Welfare Reform in West Virginia

~ *Narrative by Rick Wilson*

*The author was field staff of the West Virginia American Friends
Service Committee (AFSC) for many years beginning in 1989.
AFSC is a Quaker service organization with programs throughout
the U.S. and internationally. Rick directed the West Virginia
Economic Justice Project office out of Charleston—with the
mission of promoting peace and justice education and community
development, working in racial conflicts and labor disputes, and
leading nonviolence programs with youth. He worked extensively
on economic policy issues such as taxes, minimum wage, health
care, public services, and education. He is now retired from AFSC.*

I attended a Listening Project training of trainers in Asheville in
1994, after hearing about the process for years in my work for the
American Friends Service Committee. Since then, I have been
involved to one degree or another in several LPs in West Virginia
on issues ranging from criminal justice to human/civil rights to
food security to community development. In 1999 I initiated a
state-wide project that had a significant impact on welfare
legislation in West Virginia. It was triggered by national legislation
in 1996 that had drastically cut back on assistance provided for
low-income and disabled families and individuals. The LP was
aimed at giving voice to those who needed welfare, publicizing
their concerns and struggles, and impacting state welfare programs
by educating legislators about the reality of their situations.

 The AFSC (American Friends Service Committee) and its partner
organizations began focusing on welfare-related issues in 1997.
Our goals were both to help families get the most out of the new
system—with its significantly reduced welfare caseloads—and to

positively impact state welfare policy. As we tried to do these things, a Listening Project seemed like a natural fit, particularly since low income people were in large measure left out of the discussions and were treated and spoken of as objects. To the extent we could, we wanted to bring the voices of those directly impacted to the attention of policy makers, the media, and the public.

Interview Quotes
- *I have been to the Department of Health and Human Resources many times and feel as if I don't really matter. I'm just a customer.*
- *Treat us like people. Don't get angry when somebody doesn't understand or know everything.*
- *I've been treated like I'm stupid and worthless and like I'm not even trying to be self-sufficient.*
- *I would like to see a person who has always had money live one year on what my family does.*

Aside from those aims, we had some specific policy goals which we kept fighting for all along, viewing the Listening Project as one of several means of attaining them. These included (1) changing a state policy that denied benefits to families in which a member received SSI, (2) allowing education to count as a work activity, and (3) expanding the Children's Health Insurance Program (CHIP).

In 1998-99, the AFSC Economic Justice Project in West Virginia coordinated the effort to interview 160 past and present welfare recipients throughout the state. We partnered with many different and scattered community allies, such as the West Virginia Welfare Reform Coalition, WV Community Voices Project, Catholic Committee of Appalachia, local Head Start centers, and several social service agencies. We held several trainings around the state.

When the interviews were finished, a small group of people who had been involved in the LP gathered to review the surveys and identify key themes. Some of these points—particularly the demand to be treated like people—jumped right off the pages. We identified several themes, which provided the outline for our report.

"Life on Welfare and After" Quotes
- *Just because there was welfare reform, it don't mean my kids quit eating.*
- *I went to work and lost more benefits.... I'm barely getting by right now. I am getting help from family and friends.*
- *I am one who came from a welfare family. I want better for my kids' life. But if it was not for public assistance, I don't know what I would have done.*

We found that welfare recipients eloquently described themselves in our interviews—in ways that policy makers needed to know. So our report on the LP began by summarizing them as ordinary people who:

- Work
- Don't want to be on welfare for life
- Are not all the same
- Support changing the old welfare system
- Are concerned about abuse of the system
- Are concerned about how families will fare under welfare reform

In writing the report, I included background information about welfare reform and the project, a summary of key themes, and then a section on major themes that included introductory material and direct quotes from the people we interviewed. (See sidebars for examples of quotes from the report). Entitled Nobody Asked Us (taken from an interviewee's comment regarding welfare changes), the report made the following policy recommendations:

- **Dignity**: Treat people receiving public assistance with respect and fully inform them of their rights and options.
- **Education**: Allow motivated welfare recipients access to the full spectrum of education.

- **Spend TANF (Temporary Assistance for Needy Families) savings**: The federal block grants have resulted in millions of dollars of unspent TANF savings—due to welfare rolls dropping. That money, if not spent in various helpful ways, might result in the US Congress allocating it elsewhere.
- **Health Care**: Gaps in the health care system for low income people need to be closed, by such measures as expanding and restoring Medicaid coverage, as well as raising its threshold to give more low-wage workers health benefits.
- **Expand Awareness of Existing Programs**: Promote existing federal and state programs to many people who do not realize they may be eligible for them.
- **Work and Job Creation**: People should be paid living wages and have access to job training. Federal money already allocated could be used to create jobs useful to communities.
- **Time Limits**: The federal benefits limit of five years needs to be extended to allow families to locate adequate employment.

"Education" Quotes
- *I was told I needed to quit college and work 20 hours a week. At that point, I was one semester hour away from graduating.... I think welfare reform has made it harder on those of us who want to go back to school and get off the system.*
- *Education has taken a back seat in this county. The line from the Department is work first.*
- *The program is not designed to make it possible to attend any training or educational program.*

In the Aftermath of the Listening Project: Legislative Changes

We released the report at a press conference and gave copies to state officials and every state legislator, several national organizations, the media, various welfare-interested community groups, and as many of the people who were interviewed as we could. The subsequent press and attention the report received complemented our longer-term goal of impacting state policies.

In the 2000 legislative session, which began the month after the report was released, the legislature expanded eligibility for the Children's Health Insurance Program (CHIP) up to 200 percent of the federal poverty level and passed a law that allowed education from literacy to college level to count as a work activity for the state welfare program. Those legislative actions were exactly what we had hoped would happen.

"Children in Poverty" Quotes
- *Children are the hardest victims. If parents feel stressed... children suffer.*
- *Children get the blunt end of the deal, because other kids make fun of them.*
- *Kids grow, clothes don't.*
- *Welfare reform doesn't do anything but punish kids.*
- *If kids are hungry or embarrassed, nothing else matters—not even school.*

Today, the CHIP program threshold in WV is set at 250 percent of the poverty level and, despite negative changes to the program made by the Bush administration, the college program is still intact. Several hundred adults in the system are attending college classes and are getting the education they need to permanently escape poverty. Many more people are attending GED classes and vocational training—something the earlier program discouraged.

One recommendation of the LP was for a coordinated outreach program to help low-income people access existing programs such as the Earned Income Tax Credit. Since then, EITC outreach has become a major effort involving a number of state agencies, businesses, and community groups. We also recommended expanding supportive services to make it easier for more people to move from welfare to work.

After its release, the report made its rounds in the state and seemed to catch on pretty well. It helped inspire a series of public forums around the state in 2000-2001 on the subject of "Making Ends Meet." The forums included a discussion guide as well as a report summarizing discussions.

Some national groups used the Listening Project report for their education and advocacy efforts. The LP and related organizing efforts helped inspire the formation of a statewide welfare advocacy group of past and present recipients of public benefits, which is still active.

"From Welfare to Work" Quotes
- *I think if the state can put you to work for a welfare check, why don't they just get you a good job and forget the check?*
- *There are jobs available but some are 20 to 30 miles away and a lack of an automobile, insurance, etc. is a large problem.*
- *Work programs don't lead to jobs or skill development. They will certainly not lead to good jobs with health benefits.*
- *Job requirements are not a guarantee of real job skills.... People are not learning to be self-sufficient.*

In 2002, when families began reaching their 60-month time limit, AFSC and allies were involved in a lawsuit before the state Supreme Court challenging the cutoffs. The Listening Project report wound up being included in briefs to the court and was quoted in legal documents related to the case.

There are all kinds of Listening Projects. Some aim at conflict resolution, public education, or community organizing. Some have a very local focus, where others are broader. The Welfare Listening Project is an example of combining the LP method with other ongoing "political" strategies such as public education, coalition building, and advocacy, in order to achieve very tangible aims. Of all the ones I've been involved in, this one had by far the greatest impact in West Virginia.

Chapter 18

Healing the Wounds of Ethnic Hatred and War

~ Narrative by Corinne Bloch in the name of Center for Peace, Non-Violence, and Human Rights—Osijek

The War in Croatia

Yugoslavia, a nation in the Balkan region of SE Europe, had a history of ethnic conflict and forced unity between Serbs, Muslims, Croats, and other ethnicities. In 1980, with the death of its long-time leader, Marshal Tito, the Yugoslav nation dissolved and ethnic-based nationalism led to renewed conflict. This in turn resulted in forced ethnic relocations, killings, concentration camps, and war.

Fighting between Croats and Serbs escalated into war in the summer of 1991. Major military operations were conducted in the eastern Croatian province of Slavonia, where severe fighting lasted for 10 months. The tactic goal was to create an ethnic homogenization of the population by various means of ethnic cleansing (i.e., forced migration, massacres, concentration camps, etc.). This led, in both Croatia and Serbia, to thousands of people—mainly civilians—being wounded, killed, and missing. Almost 30% of Croatia's population—both Serbs and Croats—were driven from their homes. Several cities were completely destroyed. Many towns and villages were heavily damaged. After the war, eastern Croatia had a great number of mass graves and missing persons.

In January 1992 a cease-fire was signed, followed by five years of involvement by a United Nations mission. The tense atmosphere continued, however, with two more outbreaks of fighting in 1995, in a Croatian attempt to regain some of the lost territories. Afterwards, the first few refugees who had left Slavonia started to come back home, only to discover a tragedy left behind by the war. We pick up our story here.

The War's Aftermath

Berak: A town of 350 people, Berak is situated on one of the rare hills of the predominantly flat province of Slavonia. During the war, Berak was taken over by Serbs. Almost all of the Croats were forced to leave. Of those who stayed, most were herded into concentration camps.

In 1999, the fields surrounding Berak were still full of landmines. Social life in the village was very limited—revolving around two small shops, two churches, and a little wooden bench on the main street. After the war's end, the village and the surrounding region of Slavonia had been reintegrated by the United Nations into the Republic of Croatia. Displaced people, mainly Croats, were slowly beginning to return. Post-war tension in Berak was extremely high because practically every family in this small community could be individually linked to the violent events of the war.

Dragica Aleksa, a life-long farmer, was one of the returning Croats. After several years in refugee camps, she and her fellow returnees were eager to go back to their homes and return to normal life. But the returnees faced new traumas: destroyed homes, economic difficulties, a struggle for reintegration, and ethnic tensions.

About 10% of Berak's population was killed in the war—either in various battles or in the village's concentration camp that the Serbs had established. Dead bodies were thrown into wells or buried in undisclosed places. Thirty of them were still missing at the time that Dragica returned. She remembers:

I was looking at my former neighbors' houses. Everywhere I turned I saw that people were missing. Nothing was like it was before. I was unable to imagine reconciliation, even with my former best friend, a Serb. When she came to me, asking why I still hadn't visited her since I returned, I was able only to say, "Because you didn't help us when we had to leave."

In Berak there was no anonymity. Feelings of injustice and other strong emotions were very high. It was an extremely painful situation, with victims, perpetrators, and their families all trying to live together.

An exhumation of a mass grave in May 1999 brought some hope—but not for long. Out of the 30 missing people, only 16 were found. Anger and hatred flared up. The tension was palpable. Some Serbs even left town, for fear of retaliation. In August, the tension culminated in the tragic murder of a Serb. The situation was careening out of control.

The Organization: Centar Za Mir and the Peace Teams

The Center for Peace, Nonviolence, and Human Rights (Centar Za Mir) was founded in 1992 in Osijek, in an attempt to counter ethnic, religious, political, and ideological divisions that resulted from the ongoing war between Serbs and Croats.

In the late 1990s, the Organization for Security and Cooperation in Europe (OSCE) called on Centar Za Mir to help stop the escalating post-war ethnic hatred and violence. In 1998, Centar Za Mir, with the aid of the Life and Peace Institute in Sweden, initiated an ambitious program called "Building a Democratic Society Based on a Culture of Nonviolence—Post War Peace-Building in Eastern Croatia." The basic strategy of this program was to place multi-ethnic Peace Teams in seven East Croatia communities that were experiencing high levels of post-war ethnic tension and conflict. The Peace Teams' primary objective was to foster reconciliation and cooperation among a citizenry that was traumatized by a war that had pitted neighbor against neighbor.

But the question loomed large: How would people who had been severely traumatized by the bloody war react to these Peace Teams? Of particular concern was the anger that might be shown by the Croats towards Serbian members of the teams. The challenge was frightening, the situation dangerous.

The solution came from the Listening Project. In 1992 Herb Walters had developed a successful Listening Project in Serbia that helped diffuse escalating tensions between Serbs and Muslims in the village of Brestovac. Herb had also helped Centar Za Mir develop a pilot Listening Project that was successful in easing relations between Croats and Serbs in the city of Osijek.

Several years later, Centar Za Mir director and founder Katarina Kruhonja knew that the Listening Project was exactly the right approach for the Peace Teams. Rather than going into the various communities as experts with answers, or even as mediators, Peace Teams members would enter as listeners—friendly to all sides and respectful of the wisdom and the potential of the people themselves to find and implement solutions to their terrible situation.

Says Katarina Kruhonja:

The fact that people could freely talk about their experience, their feelings and opinions, was a completely new approach. In the very urgent and difficult situation we had to face in the post-war period, listening was probably the only possible way to enter these traumatized communities. For the Peace Teams, it was very challenging to put forth a message of peace in this dark and even sometimes dangerous atmosphere. In two locations the Peace Teams were responding to recent murders! In other villages, after the region had been reintegrated into Croatia, Serbs had barricaded the streets to prevent Croats from coming back.

The Listening Projects

In order to meet these severe challenges, a ten-week training program prepared the teams for their work. In an atmosphere of great ethnic tensions, hatred, destruction, and ethnic cleansing, the Peace Teams were the first example of ethnically-mixed groups working together to promote peace and foster alternatives to violence. *Listen to Understand* was the project's slogan, as well as Peace Teams' first goal.

During the first phase of seven different Listening Projects, some 1900 interviews were conducted in seven communities. Each project was tailored to the specific needs of its community. This approach enabled the Peace Teams to develop activities and solutions based on what was heard from the people in each community. The goal of the second phase of the work, which often began before all interviews were completed, was to encourage the participation of local individuals in the process of ongoing social change.

Centar Za Mir worked with local citizens to transform needs and ideas into specific solutions. During the third phase of the project, local residents began to create their own organizations. At that point, the Peace Teams began to play a secondary role in these communities. Centar Za Mir then supported the community groups, sometimes financially, sometimes by providing them with training.

Each Listening Project is Tailored to the Community: The Berak LP

Dragica recalls her initial encounter with the Listening Project Peace Team:

I will never forget that day when they came to my door for the first time. It was in the autumn of 1999, shortly after the murder of a Serb in Berak. It was about one year after I had returned to my village. I had lost everything in the war and had been living for seven years in a refugee camp.

I opened the door and there stood two people. They introduced themselves as part of a Peace Team working for the Centar Za Mir, based in Osijek. They said they just wanted to help. They were interested in my war experiences, in my opinion about current life in Berak, and in my ideas about how to improve life in our sad village. They said they simply wanted to listen to me and let me tell them my story. I invited them in and I started to talk. I talked and talked. I cried and cried. I could not stop myself. I needed to get rid of all the pain and questions that I had held inside for so long. They paid attention, taking notes.

Even though the interview teams were obviously of mixed ethnicity (they were identified by name tags and language) no person who was approached in Berak refused an interview. Many interviews lasted two hours or more. Very strong emotions came out, but there were no incidents.

Vesna, one member of the Peace Team, said:

At the beginning, active listening seemed very unrealistic to me. Then I realized how important it was to inquire about the real needs of people. By listening to them, we helped them to feel respected, because they had a chance to express their personal needs, as well as those of the community. Listening also helped us to build trust with the residents. They would even stop us in the street and talk to us. Most people welcomed us. In Berak, we were particularly afraid, because of the tense atmosphere; but people were delighted that there was someone ready to listen to them.

The responses in the Berak LP clearly indicated that the Croatian returnees who had been driven out of the village during the war—like Dragica—did not trust their neighbors who had remained. They also were holding onto painful memories as war victims. These feelings prevented them from communicating with those who had stayed. In contrast, for the Serbs and the few Croats and other non-Serbs who had remained in Berak, their trauma was caused by a sense of imposed collective guilt, social isolation, discrimination at the work place, loss of employment, and feelings of insecurity.

Many people talked about the difficult economic situation that had created a sense of apathy and despair—especially the problem of unemployment. There was a consensus across groups that there was a need for revitalization of the economy and a rebuilding of village infrastructure, as well as reestablishment of cultural and social life. Moreover, the Peace Teams noticed that some people showed signs of post-traumatic stress disorder, and that several families needed humanitarian, legal, and/or financial aid. In response to these needs, law experts were included in the work of the Peace Teams. They offered free legal services to people. The Center for Social Care (Caritas) and the United Nations High

Commissioner for Refugees were informed, and they both responded to the humanitarian needs in Berak.

The Croatian returnees also needed support during their mourning. They needed help searching for missing persons. The Serbs needed some sign that they were not personally blamed for what had happened during the war. The cooperation of the people who had remained in Berak was required as a precondition for peaceful coexistence. There also could be no reconciliation until Serbs and Croats started talking to each other about the war. But this would be extremely difficult, since Croats did not want to discuss these matters, even among themselves. A major question loomed: How to open communication?

In the atmosphere immediately following the Listening Project interviews, discussion on the more troublesome issue of conflict between ethnic groups was impossible. The wounds and trauma were far too fresh and deep. However, analysis of the first interviews revealed needs and possibilities for other types of activities. Since many people had spoken about the need for better infrastructure and reestablishing cultural and social life, the Peace Teams set about organizing activities for children, youth, and women. In order to build trust among Croat returnees, they tried to mobilize the citizens to participate in community actions that they themselves had suggested during Listening Project interviews.

Berak's Peace Team used the Listening Project to identify and later involve people who showed an interest in participating in activities. This included developing inter-ethnic programs and activities that could help bring people together in a safe and positive way. Many people got involved, such as the Catholic priest who made the parish house available, a young woman who started a workshop for preschool children, and a few people who led the initiative to rebuild the community center.

This community center was particularly significant, since Berak had no place where people could meet and organize events. An old destroyed house at the entrance of the village was identified and, with the financial and organizational help of the Peace Team, some motivated citizens started to work to restore the house. Once

114

rebuilt, the community center became a useable space for people. It included designated areas for workshops and lectures. Meetings were organized there, a new hunters' club started to use it, and the youth of Berak found a place to meet.

Many people—especially children—attended workshops on nonviolent communication. There were sewing and hair-styling courses, foreign language and computer classes, seminars on vegetable growing and bio-farming, environmental cleanup activities, theater performances, creative writing workshops, humanitarian actions, women's workshops on empowerment, ecumenical prayer groups, etc. There were also thematic workshops organized to meet the specific needs of people, like overcoming the victim role and taking an active role in various peace and democracy-building activities, managing conflict and trauma, and self-help seminars. The strategy was effective, and it led to the establishment of good communication and group dynamics, across ethnic lines.

After being interviewed by the Listening Project in Berak, Dragica joined a program called "Empowerment of Women to Work in the Community", which involved women from various war traumatized communities. She recalls:

I had no idea what a workshop was, but I went. Imagine my surprise when I realized that there were Serbs among us! As I introduced myself, telling them I was from Berak, a woman commented, "The village where a Croat killed a Serb two months ago." I immediately reacted aggressively. I demanded to know about the 50 Croats who had been killed during the war. Today, this woman is one of my best friends. We struggle together for peace. Things slowly change.

During the workshop, everybody had ten minutes to write something about her identity. Nobody had ever asked me such a question before. All I could think of writing was: Dragica Aleksa, Daniel's wife, Croat, Catholic. Then I thought, "That cannot be all!" In time I slowly started to feel that I could be—and do— more. I slowly became a bridge between people—visiting them, opening up dialogue, and taking part in the rebuilding of my community. But it took me almost a year to be able to enter the house of Baba Savka—the old Serb woman who was living alone in Berak, after her son had escaped to Serbia.

Today I am able to say hello to everybody in Berak. It helps to break the invisible wall between our ethnic groups. I slowly came to understand that you can start a healing process and even start to forgive someone who burned your house—but only if you come to see this person as an individual, with a name and a face. You cannot enter such a process for a whole ethnic group, however, when you don't have any idea of who you are facing.

Finally, after having worked months on rebuilding trust, the Peace Team decided that the time had come to start the process of holding a dialogue about the main problem of the village: missing persons and post-war justice.

On this very sensitive issue, the Peace Team succeeded in getting people from both ethnic groups to work together. Serbs participated because they also wanted the bodies to be found—realizing that to do so was an essential part of rebuilding community relations. A mixed delegation from the village travelled to ask the President of Croatia to put more effort into finding their missing relatives. The meeting was unsuccessful; however, it opened discussion in the community on the issue, allowing new possibilities and activities to begin. At the same time, workshops for Croatian women, including trauma treatment and bereavement support, were held.

Reconciliation is a long-term process, and active listening had to continue in order to foster further communication. Dragica understood this. In spite of her long days farming in the fields and her numerous responsibilities in the small family farm she runs with her husband, she joined a three-day active-listening course to help her establish direct communication with residents in her community. The program was called "Citizens Listen to Citizens." She began to visit everybody in Berak—both Serbs and Croats. She decided to do something for the elderly population in the village. She started to listen to their stories about their lives, their experiences, their pains, and the old customs. She helped ease their

116

loneliness and collected a wonderful set of stories, which she compiled in a book, The Stories of Berak, which was published in 2002. She recalls:

I learned so much by listening to these people. I thought they had something to give us, but I didn't expect it to be so much. Despite their having to face two wars and their lives being terribly difficult, I haven't heard any hate in their words. They always tried to point out the many small good things that happened to them. They helped me to change. I realized how important it could be for the community to share this positive experience and to remember how Berak was in the past.

The book was a success. Dragica was asked to give a presentation at the primary school in Berak and later in several nearby villages. The old traditions and wisdom, as well as the anti-war message reflected in her stories helped bring a new spirit of pride to the village of Berak—a spirit that had previously been suppressed in an atmosphere of exclusion and national tensions.

Berak 2004—A Small Light and a Big Spark

Five years after the first visit of the Peace Team to Berak, there had been no more violent incidents in the village. According to the Organization for Security and Cooperation in Europe (OSCE), the Listening Project led to a breakthrough in communication between the divided populations. As an OSCE official pointed out, one can never know how effective such an intervention really is; one can only imagine what the situation would be like if the problems had continued unchecked. In Berak, even when the exhumation of war victims occurred, the situation stayed calm, according to international police monitors.

Dragica is today one of the most committed people for peace and reconciliation in her village. In 2004 she co-founded a community organization—called Luc (Small Light)—with a Serb. Its work has been acknowledged as being of invaluable support to numerous people in Berak. She organizes many workshops for the people of her village and trains her neighbors to become, like her, peace workers in the community. Dragica is one of many in Eastern

Croatia who started to empower themselves and the others after the visit of the Peace Teams. It still incites strong emotions in her:

They really brought something very special to me and to the community. They opened a way for communication, and their commitment gave some of us the motivation to get involved in our village. They made us feel responsible for our lives and our future.

Dragica, who was nominated for the 2005 Nobel Peace Prize, says:

Though I have many plans, I have but one goal: to make the words forgiveness, reconciliation, and coexistence become more popular in my village. My biggest success is not the work I did for the community but the work I did for myself.

Beli Manistir and the Roma LP

The prejudices against Roma (Gypsies) have always been very strong in the Balkans, where they have lived for centuries and where one of the largest concentrations of Roma in Europe is found. Historically a nomadic people, the Roma have often been marginalized, have suffered human rights abuses (including being forced into slavery), and are often forcefully assimilated into the mainstream culture. Their access to education and jobs has been severely restricted.

During the war, many men in the Roma community were forcefully enrolled in the Serbian army to fight against Croats. Most of them were made to stand in the front lines, where many of them died. After the war their difficult economic situation and their already poor standing in society became even worse. Their Croat neighbors saw them as an enemy—unable to understand that the Roma had no choice but to fight with the Serbs. Thus they were targets for revenge. The new Croatian authorities and the police were not protecting them, and the humanitarian organizations were not giving them aid. They did not have personal documents, jobs, or even hope. Alcohol abuse and violence spread through the Roma community.

Dusko was in high school—only 18—when the fighting started. He was, like most of the Roma men, forced to side with the Serbs. The older men, like Dusko's father, were employed to pick up the corpses after battles. "Already at that time I hated violence. It was a nightmare," remembers Dusko.

Dusko lives in Beli Manistir, a city forty kilometers from Berak. There the Peace Teams helped local Roma establish a Roma Association. When they were asked to include Roma in the Listening Project interviews, the Peace Team immediately responded by visiting Roma settlements and then developing the Roma Listening Project. In addition to a focus on fostering reconciliation and inter-ethnic cooperation, the goal of the Roma LP was to give voice to the disempowered Roma people and help them organize to help themselves. Dusko became the coordinator for the Roma Listening Project.

Roma Listening Project questions focused a great deal on people's hopes and expectations for the future. Police protection, humanitarian aid, and education of children were the priorities they expressed. They came up with many good solutions. Additionally, they pointed out their wish to express themselves about their war experiences and their poverty. Dusko recalls:

What was most difficult was that we Roma had no idea about what our rights were, or how to initiate procedures to defend ourselves. People needed everything—from wood for heating their homes to legal assistance and insurance.

I've never been afraid, as I knew that I had nothing to blame myself for. I just wanted to forget my war experiences by helping others. I liked the way the Peace Teams welcomed me and encouraged me to get involved. I was especially interested in the possibility they mentioned of working with children. I decided to join a Listening Project training. The day after my training, I started interviewing. I began by being a recorder. It was not an easy job. Many inhabitants welcomed us, but some kicked us out—especially the Croats.

Once again, the power of listening to other people's truths, and to come to understand and respect their needs, pains, or even hate and anger, was richly rewarded. It brought us so much, especially when we started to see some concrete results that improved not only people's relationships but also their lives.

Like the other Peace Teams, the one in Beli Manastir was of mixed ethnicity, and interviews were conducted equally with all ethnic groups, although some Croats believed that the Listening Project would favor the Serbs. Dusko recalls:

When we began, a group of Croats was intimidating Serbs, trying to force them to leave the village by putting bombs in their gardens. We urged the victims to lodge a complaint with the police, which they successfully did. As a result, our reputation became even worse among the Croatian extremists. But these problems just built our motivation. We kept on trying to reach out to them, and eventually we succeeded. I especially remember a man who was one of the Croatian group's leaders. Through sheer patience, we finally convinced him to let his daughter participate in a Centar Za Mir summer camp. While there, she became very ill. We took good care of her, however, so that her father decided that we were really doing a good job for the whole community— not just biased towards the Serbs. Later on this man even started to come to our workshops!

The Listening Project and all activities of the Peace Teams had a strong focus on promoting inter-ethnic cooperation, community rebuilding, and citizen empowerment. One of the most effective activities in Beli Manastir was a greenhouse project. Serbs, Croats, Roma, and Hungarians all took part in it—starting with a seminar on how to grow vegetables and eventually building a greenhouse which they all shared. This kind of success led to development of the Baranja Civil Center (BRICC), of which Dusko became president.

In Beli Manistir and other Croatian communities, the creation of these organizations had tremendous significance, because this meant a new venture into citizen democracy and grassroots organizing.

120

Another result of the Listening Project was the empowerment of the Roma people, who launched a campaign to get their children into school. Legally, Roma children already had the right to attend school, but the basic support and funds to encourage them to go were missing. The work concentrated on getting them exposed to preschool socialization and academic preparation. Every morning in the rebuilt house by the community garden, Roma children were taught mathematics, spelling, and basic English. "Most of their parents are not educated and cannot help them with school work," Dusko explains. "If nobody gives them a boost, the next Roma generation will face the same difficulties of trying to integrate themselves into society." After seven years working with youth, Dusko was very proud to say that 30% of students in the secondary school in Beli Manastir were Roma.

BRICC also started a campaign to gain access to better water. Roma participants learned how to apply to local officials for improvements within their community. "To do it for them would be a mistake," Dusko explains. "They have to be trained to learn how to become independent, to get their own rights".

Some members of the Roma association and some individuals went to the police and the local headquarters of the Red Cross. They contacted journalists, with the result that a documentary was filmed about their life. They went on to form branches of the Roma Association of Baranja in numerous villages in the province. To further integrate themselves into their community, they joined in a community-wide program, sponsored by Centar Za Mir, called the "Days of Culture of Peace." In this they helped erase hateful graffiti messages that had been painted on walls and other places.

In Beli Manastir the situation of the Roma community still needs improvement, but things are much better. Through the empowerment of the Roma Association of Baranja, and with the help of the Baranja Civic Center and Dusko's personal commitment, the Roma have developed regular contacts with local municipal leaders and the media. Their concerns are now taken more seriously, and various initiatives have been implemented to improve their lives.

Okucani Veterans LP

Another group that was badly suffering from the war's aftermath was the returning Croatian veterans. Besides their physical wounds, many war veterans had been traumatized by their experiences. They were tormented by their remembrance of horror and violence, were haunted by guilty feelings because of their participation in war, and were left without recognition or comfort from their own people. Many of them were jobless. They faced a major struggle trying to reintegrate themselves into society.

An alarming number of veterans were committing suicide, turning to alcohol, and abusing their relationships with friends and families. Apathetic and in despair, they were trapped. Haunted by the past and unable to imagine a future, they were frozen in a terrible present.

Okucani is a village along the Croatian border with Bosnia and Herzegovina and is reputed to have housed many displaced people from both Croatia and Bosnia during the war, when people from 130 different parishes were living there. A leader of the Association of War Veterans of the Croatian War of Independence one day approached the Centar Za Mir and requested their help in Okucani. He described the problems being faced by veterans and felt that the Peace Teams might have some answers for the troubled men and their families.

Ljubica, the mother of three children, returned to Okucani after being dislocated by the war. In 1999, after participating in months of preparation and training, she became a leader of the Okucani Peace Team. This team understood the importance of the veteran's organization and responded by conducting a tailored Listening Project for them, separately visiting each branch of veterans' organizations and listening to their stories.

Most of the veterans were at first reluctant and rather suspicious about talking about their war experiences. The interviews moved forward, however, with the result that the veterans' needs became identified. Furthermore, the Peace Team convinced some of them to join a series of workshops to learn about the nature of trauma and how to begin the process of healing.

Many veterans described the importance of being listened to with a non-judgmental attitude. One recalls:

For the first time we felt that we were approached as persons, not as objects, numbers, or as patients. We could feel the understanding and the fact that our listeners wanted to get to know who we really were. It was crucial.

The interviewers also grew from the experience. Ljubica says that she learned so much about the act of good listening through the experience. She recalls:

We were listening in a new way that we had never really done before. I was able to "walk in other people's shoes"! I realized that I was listening to war veterans in a caring way, the way you listen to somebody who is important to you, like somebody from your own family. Due to the quality of our listening, the trust between everybody—the veterans, the Peace Team, and the professional trainers—developed into a deep friendship.

After interviewing the veterans, a series of seminars were organized for them. Many veterans were prejudiced and distrustful about nongovernmental organizations, so it was no easy task to get them to participate. A seminar participant recalls:

I must admit that I agreed to go to my first seminar only with great distrust. On the other hand, I was driven by curiosity. Slowly my distrust disappeared. The facilitators were such good people that I learned to accept them as my friends, and I looked forward eagerly to each following seminar. I was not alone in my suspicions. Most of those who came admitted that they were doubtful, or even thought that it would not do anything.

Ljubica recalls:

I feel that those who participated in these seminars were very brave. In such an atmosphere I very slowly began to learn about these war veterans: 16 men who I had not known before, but who, after two years of work and so much time spent together, have become like my brothers.

The seminars had a therapeutic and educational component, both of which complemented the other. Faced with their traumatic past and the terrible emotions that emerged as a consequence of their war exposure, the participants learned to observe their own responses, to engage in some relaxation techniques, and to practice other exercises for getting rid of the fears and nightmares.

During these seminars the veterans learned the techniques of nonviolent communication and creative conflict resolution. They began making positive changes in their lives, with their families and in their communities. Each participant developed his own vision of the future, became aware of his own wishes, and made plans to start anew. Results, however, did not come quickly and the work was extremely difficult!

Though they began with fear and mistrust, at the end of it all, their comments—today compiled in a booklet—testify that the seminars had completely changed their lives. Here are a few examples:

- *I now feel calm and relaxed about my future. In many ways, I have become more successful at my work, and in my ability to reintegrate into society.*

- *The seminars have opened great new possibilities. I have learned how to react in certain situations and how to solve problems that I face every day.*

- *The work during the seminars has helped me to more easily cope with the problems that have been plaguing me since the war, especially after I was wounded. The realizations that I am not alone and that other war veterans have the same problems, have helped me. I am sure that the seminars have contributed to the fact that there have been no more violent incidents or suicides of war veterans in our area.*

- *During the seminar work I got answers to the questions I had been looking for, for seven years. I have learned that not everything in life is black. There is a positive side: in our families, friends, and neighbors.*

- *I have learned what it is like to be listened to and how to listen to others. I have felt love and learned that I can love, forgive, and not hate.*

With the success of these workshops behind them, an additional workshop was later organized for the veterans' wives—to strengthen their connections with their husbands and to learn some nonviolent communication skills that they also could apply in their families and communities. Additionally, their children participated in a seven-day seminar that introduced them to these concepts, through creative workshops, learning some basic elements of nonviolent communication, and establishing mutual connections.

Said Marijana Mitrovic, one of the professional trainers who facilitated the seminars:

I felt extraordinary after the workshop cycle was completed. In my opinion, we have done a great job—and I am not a bit immodest when I say this—because the results can be seen in each person who has taken part. Working with the war veterans' wives showed us that they needed a lot of support and knowledge in order to cope with their own consequences of the war.

The success of the two-year pilot program opened up the possibility of continuing the work. The cooperation between the Peace Team and veterans' organization continued, through projects such as art therapy for the veterans and their wives. Due to the obvious positive changes in the behavior of their colleagues, several other veterans showed an interest in getting involved in these activities. Furthermore, the Peace Team helped the active members of the veterans group learn the skills and knowledge necessary for taking over this work on their own.

Ljubica comments:

*When people feel that you protect their dignity and respect them
(without attempting to dominate them), everybody can be what he
is: a human being with virtues, but also faults, accepted without
judgment. Then the process of change and restoration may begin.*

In most of the communities that had a lot of returnees, like
Okucani, the Peace Teams had little chance of success without
involving the religious community. Croatian Catholics have always
been closely connected to their religious leaders, especially during
the period when they were displaced and when they were in the
process of returning. In most cases the Catholic priest is the one
who led the return, who feels responsible for them, and who has an
important role in all aspects of life in a community of returnees.

In the Okucani Listening Project, the Peace Team knew that it was
absolutely impossible to work successfully in the community
without establishing contact with the local Catholic Church. They
found that communication between the churches was minimal.
Thus the Peace Team initiated activities promoting cooperation
and dialogue between the local Catholic, Orthodox, and Adventist
churches. The result was that a number of public lectures given by
all three priests were successfully organized, and there were many
concerts and festivities that involved all three religious
communities. It is important to understand that this represented a
radical change within these religious communities that had been
bitterly divided during the war.

These dialogues provided an opportunity for regular meetings with
local clergy and their congregations, where they began to discuss
the situation in the community, make suggestions and come to
agreements about what they could do in order to resolve conflicts,
support people in their needs, and heal their wounds. Their practice
was to discuss not only the differences, but also the similarities
between the respective church groups. They put emphasis on the
process of transforming the relationships between churches. This
approach sent a powerful message to people about the strength of a
plural society and the power of tolerance. Moreover, meeting and

discussing the situation and problems that could arise gave them an opportunity to prevent potential conflict.

Depending on their interests, some veterans gradually became involved in community work. For example, while helping organize an international youth peace camp, one of them suggested they initiate a symbolic closing of bunkers on both the Bosnian and the Croatian sides of the Sava River. They encouraged their own children to take part in the School of Peace in Mrkopalj, which gathers participants from all countries of the former Yugoslavia.

Evaluators found that the impact of the workshops on the war veterans was extraordinary. The veterans increased their self-control, and thus were able to reduce their aggression and alcohol consumption. Additionally, they found that they had: (1) fewer verbal and physical conflicts, (2) increased ability to express their needs and emotions and actively ask for support in moments of crisis, (3) improved communication with their wives and children, (4) increased interest in participating in socially useful activities and hobbies, and (5) increased self-respect and trust in their ability to communicate with others at a personal, business, and social level. When the veterans talked about what they had gained by taking part in the program, they primarily mentioned learning to be able to communicate well. In particular, they were able to more effectively interact with local government, civil associations, the Serbian community, and with other veterans' organizations.

In May 2004, the veterans who had participated in workshops decided to found their own association in Okucani: the Center for Veterans and Community. It is symbolic that the first activity organized by this new center was a trauma and community recovery workshop for wives of ex-soldiers. The mission of the association is to provide a similar recovery program for groups of war veterans and their families and to encourage and implement different projects, actions, and activities for improving the quality of life of the community in which they live.

The United Nations has included the "Community Development and Peace Building Project" implemented by the Peace Team in Okucani as being among the 10 most successful examples in the world. It has been published in the UN's book Capacity Development—Let it Happen.

Ljubica shares that this amazing experience has dramatically changed her:

Through the cooperative work and topics that we dealt with, we all changed together. After this experience my life is not the same. We are now bound together by honesty and by bonds that will hold as long as we live. We have embarked together on an unmarked path and we are the first ones to leave any traces on it. Today, several years after participating in the peace work, I can say that I understand much better what Gandhi meant when he said: "Nonviolence is the greatest power that mankind has at its disposal." For me this is now a great truth!

Civil Participation and a Sustainable Peace

These stories are illustrative of the big change and new spirit that the Listening Project has helped bring about, step-by-step, in several communities in the eastern Croatian regions of Slavonia and Baranja.

There is still a long way to go to achieve reconciliation between Serbs, Croats, and Muslims, and in the rebuilding of their communities. But the Peace Teams and their Listening Projects have opened many doors, helped heal many wounds, and have helped establish important community development efforts.

As a result of these successes, there are today a lot of Dragicas, Duskos, and Ljubicas working for peace in eastern Croatia. Free of ethnic prejudice, they work to build a new society based on civil participation and a sustainable peace.

Katarina Kruhonja, Centar Za Mir founder and director of the Peace Teams program concluded:

The Listening Project is a basic instrument in peace building, both at the level of the individual and within the community. Only when communication was opened, were people who had been separated by war and ethnic hatred able to be ready for cooperation and to become active in their community. The process helped Peace Team members reduce their own fears and prejudices, and it helped them become incorporated in the communities where they worked.

When listening is as profound as what happened in our Listening Projects, it opens the door to further developments, because it does not create the feeling of something being started and then dropped. There are no false hopes built up. Further communication and activities can be encouraged later with a follow-up effort. When the results of the Listening Project were made public in the various communities, it proved to be a very powerful tool.

By listening to people without prejudice, we helped reduce fears; and, by doing so, we found ways to open communication where there was none before. This was crucial. Step-by-step, we could feel the tensions and hate decreasing. It was an amazing encouragement. It gave us strong motivation. It has been, however, very exhausting work. The lack of debriefing opportunities at the beginning made it too heavy for some of the listeners and we had to improve their psychological support. There is no doubt that the Listening Project transformed each one of us very much.

Part IV

Listening Skills

With an open heart and mind we can experience compassion and empathy for others, including those who oppose us. With this foundation, learning and practicing listening skills becomes an expansive and joyful experience.

Chapter 19

What Makes a Good Listener? A Commitment to Our Own Personal Growth and Change

Whether we're listening to a good friend, to an antagonist, or to an opponent of our work for social change, the skills one needs to listen well are basically the same. If a person is feeling anger, resentment, confusion, or some other strong emotion, our compassionate, non-judgmental listening can help them release these feelings. Questions and listening can then guide them into a process of reflection, deepening awareness and discovery of new possibilities and solutions.

Learning various listening skills is important, but these skills can easily be lost when our minds react to another person and we become defensive, upset, or confused. How can be we bypass or overcome that shift to defensiveness or anger that can happen in a split second? There is no single answer to that question because each of us begins with different backgrounds, strengths, and emotional baggage. However, it all begins with each of us examining our lives and compassionately reflecting on how we might grow and improve personally and socially.

Motivation to Listen and Practice

Becoming a good listener also happens as each of us develops our own mental, emotional, and spiritual capacity to believe in and practice deep listening. It is this belief in the power of listening— even when someone is saying things that are upsetting to you—that helps us remain calm and trust the process without reacting. As long as you are maintaining your ability to empathize and be respectful of the other person, you will learn something, and you will most likely end the interview with a positive relationship.

Our personal belief system, including our spiritual, religious, and/or philosophical values, can be an important foundation for good listening. This is true at both the personal level, where individuals look to their own beliefs, or at the organizational level where shared goals and values enable people to work together. For example, a common understanding of Jesus's teachings about peacemaking and pastoral guidance were vital elements in the success of the Facilitated Group Listening sessions between Orthodox Serbs and Catholic Croatians who were former enemies in a bitter ethnic war. A shared belief in caring for the earth as God's creation enabled conservative Christians to express and act on their own priorities for sustainable development. A strong belief in justice and grassroots democracy has been the foundation for good listening that helped create new leadership and solutions in troubled urban neighborhoods throughout the United States. A belief in the inherent goodness in every person enabled LP interviewers to listen respectfully to people who had expressed ethnic or racial prejudice, so that in the end, some of the interviewees also expressed a need to lessen the hatred and divisions.

The skills we offer in the next part of this book will do you little good unless you practice them. After you read them, set a goal to practice them with family members or friends or people with different or opposing beliefs. The more we use the skills, the better we get at using them. The more we use them, the more we see positive growth and change. The more we experience that growth and change, the more capable we become of replacing reactivity with compassionate listening and positive change.

No one can be a good listener all of the time. Patience helps because listening can improve even when we fail to practice good listening. Rather than being upset about our mistakes, we can see them as valuable lessons—learning opportunities. Practicing our listening skills can be a wonderful journey into self-discovery and growth that over time can transform our personal lives and sometimes even the world around us.

A Good Listener Understands Basic Human Needs

Human beings have many different needs. Here, we are focusing on the needs that impact communication and human relationships.

Trust. People will not share their deep and true feelings if they don't trust us. Trust is established when: (1) we listen with respect, compassion, and empathy — even when areas of disagreement arise; (2) we are honest; and (3) we too, are open to new ideas and change.

Feeling Valued. Everyone needs to feel understood, respected, and affirmed, even when they are expressing feelings or beliefs that we do not agree with. When we are doing a good job of listening to someone, s/he will feel valued as a person with his or her own feelings, ideas, and beliefs—even if we do not agree with what we hear. Active listening includes being attentive and interested in what a person says, asking good questions, and affirming the other person. Affirmation is the act of finding and expressing to someone what we like or appreciate about them, even if it is something as simple as their smile, their love of family, a common desire for a better life, or the fact that they are good at expressing their thoughts. With good questions and good listening, we can always find some common ground with ideas, feelings, needs, or interests.

Finding our own path to change. Encourage each person's own process of reflection, introspection, and change, without giving them solutions or trying to push them into accepting our ideas. We must also accept that some people will experience little or no change, even when we are good listeners. On the other hand, sometimes it seems that way, but in truth a seed has been planted that may grow in the fertile soil of future experience.

As Listeners, we need to believe that listening is effective in bringing positive change. Historically, listening has taken a back seat to debate and defeating your opponents as a way to win and accomplish change. Yet the simple truth is that in many cases, win-lose struggles result in a winner and a loser who continue the fight with an increased level of hostility. This results in ideological, political, social, and/or religious battles that in turn lead to new forms of conflict and injustice. Yes, it's hard to listen to an opponent. But it is a very effective way of realizing change that empowers people, creates new solutions, and finds common ground. Believe in the power of listening and don't expect miracles. Just keep practicing and your skills and abilities will expand. Your faith in the process will grow as you see positive results.

Chapter 20

Wisdom and Skills in the Art of Listening

Hearing is something that we do all the time—for most of us it is involuntary. Our sense of hearing is crucial to us, because it defines how we interpret and interact with our world.

Listening happens when our eyes see the feelings communicated with the body, and we open our hearts to make room for understanding.

Listening is different from hearing …

When we simply "hear" someone, we are registering the sound of their words, but not much more. Why is this? Often our minds are distracted by our self-centered interests, making it difficult to understand what others are saying, let alone their deeper feelings and needs.

Simple, surface-level hearing is sometimes called "passive listening." There are situations where passive listening is fine. Simply hearing the directions to someone's house may be good enough, if you don't interrupt them while they are speaking. But sometimes passive listening just isn't enough. When a friend explains that she hasn't done something she promised—and you just hear her words without noticing other subtle messages—you might get reactive, angry, or upset, and miss the fact that there is a legitimate reason for her failure.

We listen best when we are attentive and keep an open mind. When we do this, we are trying to understand what is behind the speaker's words. We are trying to empathize with them (trying to walk in their shoes) so we can understand their feelings, needs, and circumstances.

In the example given above, let's say that, instead of just hearing the words, you might notice your friend is looking overwhelmed and stressed out. Maybe that helps you to remember that she has recently been through a family crisis. That attentiveness can open you up to having some compassion for her, rather than getting angry. As an active listener, you can take a further step and ask your friend a couple of questions that help you better understand what is behind her words. She will most likely appreciate your questions (if they are asked with sensitivity) and take the opportunity to share her feelings with you.

Active listening is an important skill in both psychology and counseling. Carl Rogers was one of the great pioneers of using active listening to help people deal with emotional, psychological, and life issues. Rogers found that rather than analyzing someone and giving them answers on ways to improve their life, it was better to listen deeply, empathize, and ask good questions that could help a person go through a process of self-reflection and understanding. Rogers and many other renowned therapists found that this process enabled people to tap into their inner wisdom and find their own solutions; and because these solutions came from within themselves, they were often very effective.

What Listening is Not

A common misconception is that we can effectively communicate by impressing the other person, or by out-talking or out-arguing them. How often do we find ourselves listening to the other person with just enough attention to be waiting for that split second when they pause, to take advantage of that tiny opening that allows us an opportunity to tell them the truth, or put them in their place with our incisive argument and keen wit?

Communication through listening is not about trying to manipulate or push someone into seeing our truth. Too often, we listen to the other person with the selfish goal of changing them or of convincing them that their reasoning is erroneous. This communication pattern is forceful, judgmental, and contentious, and it sends a message that we are really turning a "deaf ear" to them. The result is that any sense of separation we had when we started is escalated. Even if we are successful in manipulating someone into accepting our beliefs, forced change at best will be short-lived and might simply result in a later hardening of a person's position. No one likes to be pushed into changing his or her beliefs.

But is it OK to want the other person to change?

On the other hand, we want to make it clear here that we feel it is sometimes quite justifiable to wish that someone you are listening to will change—particularly when they might be saying harmful and/or negative things. If we listen to someone make a racist comment, for example, it is appropriate to wish that they might change in a positive way. The key here is that our hope that this person will change their racist views must not interfere with our ability to accept them as a person. We must find a way to listen and establish a relationship of trust with them, in order that the door to change may open. Building this mutual respect and understanding is our first and most important goal in the communication process. Once that foundation is established, we will be much more effective in dealing with racist beliefs or other negative and harmful positions.

Of course, it's also crucial to remember that we must remain open to change ourselves. Nothing is gained if either party maintains a rigid stance. For example, in the course of listening to someone expressing the belief that jobs are more important than saving the environment (if we feel quite the opposite), we might experience a change of heart if we begin to understand that this person sees their family's survival to be at stake. We can come to understand that our desire for a healthier environment must accept that working toward that direction may entail our opening up to a more complex and complete understanding of the situation. It probably is not nearly as straightforward as we might have wanted it to be.

So, communicating with someone for the purpose of creating positive change is quite appropriate. Forcing or manipulating that change is not, however. Ultimately our goal is to foster a communication process where both parties can feel safe, and where both are able to reflect and explore new possibilities together.

Every person in this life has something to teach me—and as soon as I accept that, I open myself to truly listening. — Catherine Doucette

Listening Barriers

Although good listening skills can be cultivated, barriers can make the process more difficult. It is worth describing a few of these obstacles, so we that we can better recognize when we are banging our head up against one without knowing it.

Prejudice and stereotyping that we may have unconsciously adopted from our environment can build formidable walls against listening. The key to working with this conditioning effectively is to learn to recognize the presence of our own stereotypes and deliberately prevent them from influencing our conversations.

A second societal influence that creates barriers to listening is our tendency to be in a hurry. We are an instant-gratification culture that demands immediate answers and quick results. Listening, however, asks us to take a little time. To listen really well we have to pause, ponder what we've just heard, and then ask some questions to be sure we understand. If we don't give ourselves that little window of time and the spaciousness of silence, real listening can't happen.

Many times we find ourselves a little rigid and inflexible in our interactions with others. We think we know the answer and have already closed our minds on the issue at hand. We have staked out our position and refuse to budge. Is there anyone of us who has not felt this way? Does listening stand much of a chance when we do this?

Another common barrier that we seldom recognize is a discrepancy in the meaning of the words we use. Words often convey quite different meanings to people raised and educated in different circumstances or cultures. Even when we think we are "speaking the same language," we can discover that words have diverse meanings and connotations for each party. Such differences in interpretation can build rock-hard walls and misunderstanding.

Of course, one of the greatest impediments to good listening is our own talking. How often do we dominate conversations or interrupt repeatedly because we are so compelled by our own feelings and message?

Finally, perhaps the most hidden but serious barrier to good listening is our own fears. We all carry the fear of failure, of not being good enough, or of being misjudged by others. We harbor vague fears of the unknown and all sorts of other fears that we learned as a child. This burden of fears has a tremendous influence on our feelings and actions. When one of our fears takes hold of us as we are trying to listen, we can quickly close down and become defensive. We simply cannot listen well when this happens, because we unconsciously feel the need to defend ourselves, in order to maintain our long-held sense of who we are. Our life-long task is to learn to recognize and reduce our fears so we don't take things personally.

Listening is a sacred act ...

If we take an honest look at ourselves, we can see that we sometimes fall into some of the above "not-listening" traps. We don't always pay attention. Being a good listener begins with showing the other person some respect. If we don't believe that who they are and what they have to say is worthy of our attention, we cannot communicate.

Good listening is, in fact, an act of love. It is a sacred act that we do for one another. It is a very simple but profound act of acceptance and compassion. When we really listen, we are seeking to understand the other person, to open to their truths and insights. It is humbling to admit that we don't possess all the answers or all the truth. When we open up and listen, we connect with the other person on a deep, heart-centered level.

When we listen well to another person, we are helping to reduce fears and misunderstandings we both may have of each other. As our mutual fears and misconceptions decrease, tension and mistrust are reduced or even eliminated. Then it becomes much less likely that we will angrily confront each other or get into conflict. Good listening opens up an inviting and harmonious space between us. There we can soften and become more flexible. We can experience a freedom that allows us to become vulnerable to each other as the barriers of suspicion begin to melt. Our compassion and mutual sense of humanity grow.

As we further build trust by practicing good listening, even more space begins to open up, and we find we have some common ground with the other person—a shared place that we could not see before. Our feelings of empathy and acceptance are even further strengthened. Yet even more space opens, where we find both ourselves and the other person seeing new possibilities and experiencing creative insights. Joining each other on that common ground opens up new paths and directions for us both. This loving act of listening has brought wisdom to the process, engendering positive change in each of us and transforming our relationship.

Listening and Nonviolent Social Change

When nonviolence is omitted as people work for social change, major misunderstandings can occur, resulting in widening gaps and polarization. Each side finds more and more reasons why their opponent is wrong and they are right. Each side demonizes the other, turning them into a despised enemy. Having an enemy seems at first to make things clear and simple, because it's easy to get riled up about those nasty people on the other side. It's easy to win recruits to your side. However, this demonizing also personalizes the conflict by transforming an issue into a person-to-person battle, wherein each side is more likely to take rigid positions. The potential for creative solutions is decreased, and the potential for escalated conflict and even violence is increased.

When active listening is brought into the picture, however, the opposing sides have an opportunity to understand one another and to experience each other's humanity. The possibility for resolving the conflict is increased. Active listening has been a natural and important part of many social change movements. Perhaps the best example in the U.S. is the work of Dr. Martin Luther King, Jr. His nonviolent civil-rights work was deeply rooted in his passion for human rights, as well as in his ability to listen to and understand the fears, the needs, and the potential of white Americans. As Dr. King clearly demonstrated, active listening can be a spiritual practice that helps us understand the potential of every human, and to act under the influence and power of love.

An Example of Deep Listening

The active listener in this exchange is AL. The speaker is SP.

SP: Those Mexicans need to go back where they came from.

AL: Are you angry with Mexicans who have been moving into our community?

SP: Yeah! They're using welfare and taking jobs from us. And they don't even want to speak English.

AL: I don't know much about that. What welfare programs do you think they are using?

SP: Well, they just use all the welfare programs, and nobody even cares that they are illegal. Those are my tax dollars. Why should I pay for someone who has committed a crime?

AL: You mean the crime of coming here illegally?

SP: Yes.

AL: Are you still working at the Waverly plant?

SP: Yes.

AL: How is work going for you now?

SP: (Speaks at length about his work, and the listener affirms him).

AL: Do you think there are any benefits to having some immigrants from Mexico here?

SP: Maybe, if they came legally.

AL: What benefits do you think have come from legal immigrants?

SP: Well, some of them are hard workers.

AL: Have you seen Mexicans who are hard workers?

SP: Well, yes, but that's beside the point. They may be hard workers, but they might be taking the job of a hard-working American citizen. If they came legally and pay taxes, then they deserve to be treated fairly.

AL: It sounds like you're not anti-Mexican, but you are against illegal immigration?

SP: Absolutely.

AL: There are some studies that say even illegal immigrants end up putting more into the economy then they take out. Have you heard any such thing?

SP: No. I don't believe it.

AL: Have you had any direct experience with Mexicans?

SP: Well, there are some Mexicans who work at the plant where I work.

AL: Are some of them good workers?

SP: Yes, they are. But I don't know if they are legal or not.

AL: Do you know anything about them?

SP: Not really. Well, I know one of them has a kid, because I've seen his wife and kid come to pick him up after work.

AL: From what I've learned so far, I've found that a lot of Mexican immigrants come from really poor situations where they can hardly keep their families alive, so they come here in desperation. It seems that global free trade was supposed to make things better for everyone, but it doesn't seem like that's worked the way we were told it would.

SP: That's for sure. It's made things worse here; that's for sure.

AL: Are you ever worried about your work?

SP: Damn right! Everywhere I look some plant is closing down and the work is going to other countries.

AL: Yeah, this global economy seems to be hurting everyone. I sure hope you don't lose your job, and I'd be the first one to fight against them closing Waverly. How is your family doing?

SP: (Person speaks about is family and some of the highs and lows of what they are experiencing).

AL: Sounds like you've done a great job of providing for your family. I guess one of the problems is that so many Mexicans feel they have to come here to survive.

SP: Yeah, they are pretty poor down there.

AL: I agree with you that the current situation isn't good and it would be good to have a system that was more fair and just for everyone: both U.S. citizens and Mexicans. One of the problems seems to be that we can't ever come up with a really good and comprehensive immigration reform plan. Why do you think that is?

SP: It's political. Politics gets in the way, and the Democrats and Republicans can't agree on anything. I'm tired of this mess.

AL: Me too! You know, you and I are family men, and sometimes I really feel for some of the Mexican families who have been here for a long time now and have been working hard and then their families are torn apart when the father is snatched up by authorities and his family is left not even knowing what's going on.

SP: I don't know about that. There needs to be some way to keep the families together.

AL: I agree with you. I appreciate having such a good talk. Immigration is a tough issue and it would be great if more people could talk about it like we have instead of just arguing.

SP: Yeah.

Authors Note: This conversation is one that could easily be occurring within a Listening Project interview. If that were the case, then additional questions might be asked and the interview might end in this way:

AL: Well, I told you earlier about our organization and how we are interviewing people like you because we feel there is a need for some changes in what's currently happening with free trade policies and immigration. We want to hear from workers like you because we think your ideas and feelings are important. We are also interviewing immigrants to better understand what's going on with them. Then we'll have a report about what we learn. Your name won't be in that report unless you've given permission for that to happen. You sure did give some interesting answers to my questions. Are you interested in getting our report?

SP: Sure, why not.

The Listening Process—Skills to Practice

There are many available training programs that teach people good listening skills. Listening Project training prepares organizations and individuals to be skilled in addressing vital community issues. Here we share listening skills offered at one of our training sessions. This comes from our many years of experience. It's important to understand that none of these skills stand on its own, for listening is an unfolding process.

Begin with empathy

What one is trying to do in order to listen well is to put attention to the words, while simultaneously trying to understand what is underneath the words. To do this we have to empathize with the person—as the old saying goes: "Walk a mile in their shoes." And there is no better way to walk in someone's shoes than to ask questions and listen in a way that enables you to understand the fullness of their feelings, experiences, values, fears, hopes, needs, intentions, and ideas.

Cultivate a positive attitude...

...about the person to whom you will be listening before you even begin a conversation. Here are a few steps to take:

Prepare yourself mentally and spiritually to be a non-judgmental, caring, and empathetic listener

Listen with the heart rather than the intellect. In other words, practice empathy and listen for feeling and meaning. This will help you reduce defensiveness and establish a positive, trusting relationship with the other person.

Don't be emotionally attached to a particular outcome of your listening and dialogue

It's important to really want to hear what someone has to say, rather than trying to force them to change. We can remember that it is compassion, forgiveness, and life experience that best foster personal change in others and in ourselves.

Don't define or judge someone by their beliefs. Believe in the human potential for good

Beliefs are learned behaviors that come and go. Harmful beliefs or attitudes often come from negative life experiences. Develop an attitude of humility, compassion, and faith in the human potential for growth and change. Don't be afraid that accepting someone will fortify beliefs that stand in the way of positive change. Remember that you are accepting the person, not necessarily all their beliefs. Through our acceptance, we are simply recognizing that there is more to this person than their perceived apathy or prejudice. We are recognizing their inherent worth and their potential to change and help create a better world. It can also help to look back to some of our own past beliefs that we now see were harmful.

Open yourself to change

If you really listen, you cannot help but increase your understanding of the other person. Whether or not your basic perspective on the issues you are addressing changes, your heart and mind may open, so that how you respond to differences will probably be changed.

Once you are engaged in a conversation, the following listening skills can build trust, increase communication, and deepen your understanding of the other person:

Take time to establish a human connection

If you're meeting with someone to discuss a problem, don't get right down to business. Make a person-to-person connection first and find common ground. Ask a few introductory, easy-going questions. Be genuine and don't do this to manipulate, but to help each of you relax and get a taste of your common humanity.

Be attentive to the other person

Let them know with your words and body language that you are interested and caring about what they have to say. This includes:

Affirm the other person and find common ground

Affirmation means finding and highlighting things we like or appreciate about a person. It is one of the most essential elements of good listening because it is so vital to building trust. But it only works if the affirmation is genuine. Even if you have very little in

146

common with the other person you can always find something to affirm, whether it be something as simple as their smile, their love of family, a common desire for a better life, or the fact that they are good at expressing their thoughts.

In seeking common ground, remember: Even if you disagree with 90% of what a person says, you can begin by focusing on the 10% you do agree with. For example, one person made racist remarks and also went on to talk about how as a poor, uneducated rural woman, she had suffered many injustices. Rather than focus on the disagreements and racist statements right away, the listener focused on the person's feelings about injustice. This common ground enabled a relationship of trust to develop between the two people, and it enabled the listener to more effectively bring up issues of racial justice and possible solutions.

Pay attention to body language — yours and the other person's

Whether a person's body is tense or relaxed tells you a lot about how they are feeling. Your body language is important too; they will respond or react to the positive or negative body language seen in you. A relaxed body and appropriate eye contact are useful. Also, be mindful of crossing your arms, as that often comes across as a defensive posture. Facial expressions and vocal responses should let them know you are really listening.

Acknowledge, repeat, or summarize the other person's statements

Saying something like "uh-huh" when a person is speaking is a way you can acknowledge what they are saying. Encourage them to continue and go deeper, without interrupting or stopping their train of thought. Repeating or summarizing what they say assures them that you really are hearing them. Also, they can then correct you if you didn't get their meaning. The truth is: people need to feel understood, far more than they need you to agree with them.

Listen for and encourage the expression of feelings, needs and beliefs

A statement like, "You seem really upset by what happened," encourages a person to talk about his upset feelings. People need to share even their most negative feelings before they can begin to look at new possibilities. Focus on and try to understand the feelings and needs that are underneath a person's attitude or position on an issue. Basic needs often show themselves in people's hopes or fears. For example, a person in a troubled community may say they are not interested in helping to change things. By asking some questions, however, you might find that the reason for this is that their efforts to affect change have failed in the past and they're afraid of getting hopes up, only to have them dashed once again.

Ask clarifying questions

Additional questions can help you better understand people's thoughts, ideas, beliefs, feelings, and needs. For example, you might ask, "When did that happen to you?" or "Do you think people are still upset about that?" or "Help me understand what you want to have happen and why." You can also ask questions that might give the speaker an opportunity to clarify and possibly re-think what they are saying, like, "So you think dialogue between the two groups wouldn't do any good at all? Can you see any way in which it could help?"

Encourage people to share their stories

Telling a story is often the easiest way for a person to open up and share thoughts and feelings. People sometimes don't feel comfortable talking about complex or difficult issues, but they can enter into those same issues through telling a story that relates in some way to their lives and histories. Stories provide an invaluable look into people's life experiences—including their hopes, fears, values, and beliefs.

Offer information or ideas and ask the person to share their feelings about what you offered

This includes new information or ideas that may stimulate them to consider new ideas and possibilities. It is best to offer information in a questioning manner, which puts the focus on their thoughts and feelings about the information you have provided. For example, when LP listeners asked residents of an Appalachian mountain community to share their feelings about studies revealing toxic waste in local wells, many people began for the first time to connect family health problems with the water contamination. As a result of this deeper reflection, some residents who had previously not wanted to stir up trouble, decided it was time to take a stand.

Encourage people to think creatively and to offer possible solutions or leadership

Always treat people as if they are a part of the solution – even if they have thus far been a part of the problem. Timing is important as many people need to discuss their fears and concerns before they can start talking about solutions. When you ask a question such as, "How might we help solve this problem?", you are indicating you really want to know what they think and that you believe in their ability to help solve a problem. If they don't have an answer, give them another opportunity later in the listening session. When they do give a suggestion, make sure to affirm their participation even if the solution isn't one you agree with. If that's the case, you can continue asking questions and exploring other possible solutions.

Share your ideas or feelings

This is not usually done in a Listening Project, or it happens in a very careful and limited way. However, in personal situations, sharing your thoughts or feelings may well be appropriate. If you encounter someone who is speaking or acting in a way that seems dishonest or unfair, and you feel the need to defend yourself, try not to respond confrontationally so you can keep communication open. You can, for example, share your feelings about how the other person's behavior is affecting you. But do so with care, compassion, and humility. It is helpful to use "I" statements. Here are some examples of how this can be done:

- *"I understand that you don't agree with my position on this issue, but I'd like not to make this personal, and see if we can get to a place where we can respectfully listen to each other."*
- *"I understand that you have some really strong feelings about Muslims, but it's hurtful to me when you condemn all Muslims, because a good friend is from Pakistan. What are your fears about Muslims?"*

Practice empathy

Yes, we are repeating ourselves, but it's because empathy is the most important listening skill. It teaches us to flex our heart muscles and become more compassionate. We go beyond understanding a person's position to identifying with their feelings, thus relating to them on a much deeper level and cultivating a sensitive, respectful relationship. For example, a person might say that he supports the death penalty. If you are anti-death penalty, you might have a hard time accepting this position. However, you might more easily empathize, understand and accept his fears about crime and the safety of his loved ones. His need is for some kind of assurance that there are other, better options for ensuring the safety of his family. Therefore, as a good listener, you can demonstrate empathy for his need to protect his family, and at some point you could ask him to share his ideas on alternatives to the death penalty.

Empathy Exercise

If we were to choose the most important listening skill, it would probably be empathy. The following exercise can help you develop your own empathy skills.

1. Think of a person with whom you have or had an unresolved conflict.

2. Think of the particular position they took, or of a statement they made which you deemed negative or unfair.

3. Get a piece of paper and divide it down the middle lengthwise, so there are two long columns. First, write down all the negative feelings you have about them. Don't worry, it's okay to list any and all negative feelings—just let them out. It's part of this exercise. Put this list on the left side of the paper.

4. Now take time to look at what might be underneath what they said or did. This might include:

- *Why might they be feeling defensive?*
- *What might they want to defend?*
- *What positive hopes and desires might they be fighting for?*
- *What fears or insecurities might they be carrying?*
- *What misunderstandings might they have?*
- *What past experience(s) might they have had that would contribute to their insecurity or fear, or that might result in their saying something like this?*

Write all these on the right side of the paper, or just list them in your mind.

5. Take time to reflect on your responses to the questions in number four. Try to open your heart to this person so you can better understand them and create an atmosphere where some positive communication can occur.

6. If you do this on paper, look at each list and ask yourself the following questions:

- *"If I respond to this person with my mind on the negatives, how will this affect our communication and relationship? How might they respond?*

- *"If I respond with empathy {the list on the right}, how will*

151

that affect our communication and relationship? How might they respond?

Now ask yourself:

- Which way will be more likely to result in positive communication?

Preparing for a Possible Difficult Encounter with Another Person

Take the time to try this approach. It will make a difference. After you've done it several times, you can simply do it in your mind without writing things down. Remember that in the conversation, your first task is to keep your cool—don't let anger or frustration dominate your feelings. As often as you need, pause and take deep breaths.

1. **Basic human needs.** Reflect on how each of the basic human needs described earlier applies to the other person and to you. In some cases, you may not know for sure, but it's OK to reflect on possibilities. You might check to see if you're on the right track by asking a good question when you meet.

2. **Affirmation.** Think of as many affirmations as you can for the other person. Write them down. Of course, you may have some things you don't like about the other person, but for now, just put those negatives to rest. Affirm yourself as well—especially those parts of you that will help you be non-defensive and a good listener.

3. **Empathy and self-understanding.** Do the empathy exercise—focusing on the person you will be meeting. Do step 4 for yourself. This will help increase your self-awareness and humility.

4. **Questions.** Think of questions you might ask the other person—questions that might help you better understand and empathize with them. Questions are a wonderful replacement for the "convincing" statements we often use—that rarely convince but often make the person defensive and argumentative. For example, instead of saying, *"Having this group home in your community won't be a problem because the kids are always supervised;"* with *"What are your concerns about having this group home in your neighborhood?"* And later: *"What could be done to reassure you that having the home here won't negatively impact your family?"*

5. **Be clear that your primary goal is not to change the other person.** Rather, it is to create a positive communication relationship that will leave the door open to further exploration, reflection, and new possibilities.

PART V

Other Ways to Apply Listening to Personal and Social Change

> Some will think this is a far-fetched idea. But as we look at the massive failures and terrible consequences of war and aggression, along with issues of social justice and the environment, we believe it's time for new ideas and solutions. The possibilities are as great as the creativity, commitment, and strength of 'we the people'.

Chapter 21

Facilitated Group Listening (FGL)

Facilitated Group Listening starts with a large group of people who have come together to listen and dialogue on a particular problem or issue. The group listening does not begin until everyone agrees to a verbal contract. This contract includes rules and guidelines that protect each person's right to express their thoughts and feelings without being disrupted, challenged, or criticized. Then participants meet in small groups—usually four to a group. Trained or experienced facilitators guide each small group and also help the group maintain their commitment to their verbal contract. This helps participants with differing or opposing beliefs engage in safe, respectful dialogue that increases mutual understanding.

Facilitated Listening also encourages participants to share creative ideas and solutions that can lead to further education and action on important or difficult issues. Large group discussion follows the small group listening with the focus being on personal and group plans for follow-up action.

What follows is an inspiring account of Facilitated Group Listening that was used in conjunction with the Peace Teams Listening Project on ethnic conflict and reconciliation in Croatia.

FGL in Croatia

"I used to have nothing but fear and hostility toward Serbs. My heart is still heavy with the pain, killings, and suffering caused by 'Serbo', the mock name I have used for all Serbs. But today I can say that I have met Serbo and I have seen him as a human being. We have listened to each other and I can even say I like him. Now I can return home with a new understanding and a new desire to work for reconciliation, something that before I could not imagine feeling."

These are the words of a Croatian woman who participated in a two day Facilitated Group Listening Session between Catholic

Croatians and Orthodox Serbs in Vukovar, Croatia. The event was organized by Lidija Obad, director of "Conflict Resolution Training for Religious Communities and People." CRTRCP is a joint project of the Center for Peace, Nonviolence, and Human Rights in Osijek, Croatia, and the Center for Strategic and International Studies in Washington, D.C.

In 1991, Vukovar's population of 44,000 was approximately 47% Croat and 32% Serb. During the war Vukovar was surrounded, bombarded, and under siege by Serb forces for four months. In November 1991, Serb forces mounted a final assault and took control of the city. 15,000 Croatian residents were evicted or imprisoned. The destruction of Vukovar was as complete as the heavily bombed cities of WWII.

Vukovar lay in ruins at the time of our facilitated listening sessions. Many Serb residents were displaced from their former homes in Croatia or were refugees from Bosnia. They, too, were driven from their homes by ethnic hatred and war. Many Vukovar residents lived in bombed-out remains of homes, or in the few surviving ones, or in the very few homes rebuilt in the past years. Residents of Vukovar had little sense of security. The city was still surrounded by barbed wire and land mines. Travel into Vukovar was restricted by the U.N.

In retrospect it is amazing that in the midst of so much pain and trauma, our Facilitated Listening sessions were so successful in opening dialogue and reconciliation. The potential for religious leadership in reconciliation was evident throughout the Vukovar listening sessions. Priests and lay people alike were able to draw upon scripture and other religious teaching to find a faith-based foundation for reconciliation. Father Branko Kosec led the opening prayer, referring us all to "God's command in the Lord's prayer: 'Forgive us our trespasses as we forgive those who trespass against us...' God is love and truth, mercy and faithfulness, and we must look to St. Francis to advocate peace, forgiveness, and reconciliation," said Father Branko.

The primary listening sessions occurred in small groups with roughly equal numbers of Croats and Serbs. One participant spoke for others at the conclusion of our FGL sessions. "We have come to the realization that we have been influenced in so many ways to just see each other as Chetniks and Ustaza. These are images that bring fear of one another into our hearts; the media and the politicians and the war itself have made these images of fear and hatred strong in our minds. But now we have new images and we see each other as people who have suffered. Now I think that it is possible that we might live together in peace once again."

FGL definitely takes less time and resources than a Listening Project. Another strength of FGL is that it can be held with a large group of participants who can form small groups in which to listen to one another. On the other hand, the ability to reach out to people who won't or don't come to a group event can be lost. While FGLs can facilitate invaluable deep sharing, the intimacy of one-on-one interviews can enable people to be more open and honest with their feelings. LP interviewees also have more time to explore their feelings and speak individually. Ideally LPs and FGL work well together. Consultation with a LP/FGL trainer can help you decide what is best for you.

Chapter 22

Community Meals, Listening Booths, and Circles

~ Narrative by Caite Caughey

What could happen if we listened to one another? What could we dream up together? How might listening impact our neighborhood?

These questions guided our grassroots organization in Omaha, Nebraska — inCOMMON — to the Listening Project in late 2009. A year earlier in September, 2008, our Director of Neighborhood Development, Brittany Hanson, in collaboration with the local faith communities, organized the Park Avenue Community Meal. The meal is a weekly gathering space for neighbors to share a warm meal and conversation. It is open for lunch and hospitality every Saturday afternoon, and usually brings 200 to 300 neighbors around the table. Sixteen neighborhood faith communities support and sustain this project as a way to engage deeper with their neighbors and collaborate across faith traditions and beliefs.

Over the course of two years, inCOMMON recognized a great potential for creative advocacy that was revealed by the wealth of stories and ideas that have been shared at the Community Meal. This inspired new projects. The first venture was a neighborhood photography project that focused on visual depictions and snapshots of neighborhood culture. Brittany collected photography depicting everyday neighborhood images. These photographs are currently on display at a local church. Our next step was listening more intently and finding a project that valued listening, storytelling, and community development. The Listening Project sees all people as part of the solution, not the problem. This was exactly what we needed in the neighborhood. A few willing neighbors started organizing the project with inCOMMON, and in February 2010, the group outlined their goals.

The group wanted to create safe spaces, just like the Park Avenue Community Meal, where people might stop and share their stories and ideas. In May 2010, Herb Walters trained twelve Listening Project organizers at inCOMMON. A few weeks later the organizers began listening around the neighborhood. However, we didn't use the usual interview model of going to people's homes for our interviews.

Listening Booths were our first method of conducting neighborly interviews. This included two chairs set up in the neighborhood where people gather or intersect. One chair is for the listener and the other for someone willing to talk. We had no shortage of people who were delighted to share their ideas and stories with us.

Listening Circles provided opportunities for group dialogue similar to the Facilitated Group Listening program. In the circles, neighbors are exploring their own stories and experiences and their connection to the neighborhood. The project is sprouting many ideas for our neighborhood as well as opening doors for collaboration with other organizations. We are working with Neighbors United, Omaha Table Talk, Progressive Omaha, and Creighton University students who will be participating in our Listening Project. Another new partnership is with the City of Omaha! Our Mayor just started the Cities of Service Program and we are looking for ways to collaborate with volunteers across the city.

We've already heard a lot about community priorities and challenges, community leadership, suggestions for change, and personal reflections in the first month. Following the interview portion of our project, we hope to screen a short film highlighting as many of the interviews as possible, as well as host summits and gatherings where we can share the interviews as an educational tool that can lead to cooperative community action.

A Few Clips from our Listening Booth:

Guiding Questions:

159

- Tell me about your neighborhood. What is it like?
- If there were a group of people in your neighborhood working for positive change, would you like to be involved?
- What sort of things would you like to work on?

Sample of Responses:

- *"When I first moved here I thought the neighbors would be mean, but they were really nice. That is the best thing about the neighborhood, the people."* Rajanae Birge
- *"There's a lot more need for people to be involved, and build relationships most of all. Because like the song says 'people need people,' and they need someone that wants to listen."* Modesto Olivo
- *"There needs to be more for the youth, they need an outlet to be kids."* Gene Moore
- *"There is a lot of potential for things to happen right now in this neighborhood. That is why we moved here, because it is a neighborhood in transition."* Brian Gladstone
- *"If you can't sit out in your front yard and see your kids running up and down the street with the neighbors, then something's wrong with the neighborhood."* Reuben Thornton, Sr.
- *"I don't care if you're male or female or somewhere in between, everyone has something to say."* Larry Graves
- *"Now we got our own place. It's a slum house, but oh well, at least it's ours."* Traci Laney

Yes, we have had some negative responses to the questions. People have especially mentioned concerns about affordable housing, problems with landlords, concerns about accessible transportation (many people struggle to get to and from their jobs). People have mentioned the English-Spanish language barrier being a large deterrent that keeps the community from working together more cohesively. Other topics mentioned have been about the drug trade and prostitution. However, overall we receive responses in the camp of "we think things are turning around, or at a turning point." For updates on our project: www.incommoncd.org

Chapter 23

Three Options for Getting Your Feet Wet

If you are a group that is concerned about a community problem (or a regional, state or national issue), but you are not an organization with resources to both conduct a Listening Project and conduct follow-up organizing and action; here are two simpler listening methods that enable you to give it a try without making the big commitments of a Listening Project.

Informal Listening Without Pre-Determined Questions

One approach is to engage in informal active listening with neighbors, friends, or people who might have some interesting perspectives or information on the issue(s) that concern you. In this case you might think about the kinds of questions you want to ask people, but the listening is not in the form of an interview with established questions—more like a neighborly discussion. This will help you have a better understanding of people's perceptions, concerns, and ideas related to the problem. It might also give you an initial idea of how serious a problem might be and if there are people interested in working together on it. This informal type of listening is a great experience for anyone. If you do a good job of listening, you'll be surprised how fascinating and fun it can be.

Listening to Learn: Planned Listening with Pre-Determined Interview Questions

If an organization or group does not possess the resources to conduct a LP and do the follow-up organizing and action, there can still be significant benefits that come from a coordinated series of interviews in the community. For example, you might want to better understand the concerns of residents, open channels of communication, strengthen the resources of the group, or lay the foundations for a possible future LP or organizing effort. What's important here is that you be completely up-front with the people you interview, letting them know that you don't have the organizational ability to respond to the issues and problems that might be discussed. Instead, this is a first step in finding people who might want to work together to respond to community needs. This was the case with the Winchester LP in Chapter 12.

In the mid-1980s participants in a peace walk across Massachusetts conducted a Listening to Learn project. With planned questions and listener training behind them, members of this peace group took time in several communities to listen to people and ask questions that were crafted to get people's perspectives on nuclear issues, as well as other matters impacting their lives. What happened in many cases was that the activists were changed through their listening. One participant interviewed a Vietnam veteran who was living in poverty. He was unable to find work, his kid was sick, his family was falling apart, and he knew that he and his family might one day become homeless. "After listening to him, I realized I could never continue being the kind of peace activist I've been thus far," reported the listener. "After listening to and feeling the despair I felt today, I know now that I have to pay attention to the things that are coming down on people's lives. That man can't be thinking about the nuclear arms race when his own life is falling apart and there's little justice for the poor."

Listening to a Perceived Opponent or "Enemy"

A more complex "Listening to Learn" project was at that time called the Contra Listening Project. It was conducted by Herb Walters and Carol Lathrus in 1988. At that time Contra fighters (Nicaraguans who were funded and armed by the U.S.) were attacking communities throughout Nicaragua. Their goal was to destabilize and overthrow Nicaragua's Sandinista, which was viewed by the Reagan administration as being a socialist threat in the Americas. Others in the U.S., including organizations that advocated peace in Central America, viewed the Sandinistas as legitimate representatives of the Nicaraguan people who were working hard to prosper after being ruled by the oppressive

Somoza regime. The Sandinistas were demonized by the Reagan administration and many peace activists did the same to the Contra, who were seen as pawns for misled U.S. intervention.

The goal of the Contra Listening Project interviews was to get a deeper understanding of who the Contra fighters were—the common soldiers, not the leaders. We asked them questions about their reasons for joining the Contra as well as the morality of their war against their own people. Herb hoped that this listening would reveal possibilities for greater understanding, justice, and reconciliation for the common people who were doing the fighting for leaders on both sides.

What was learned through the Contra Listening Project was shared through numerous articles in magazines and journals of local, regional, and national peace organizations. Reader responses ranged from one reader being "utterly appalled" and asking if we were a "front for the CIA and Reagan," to another who felt the Contra project had raised some of the most important questions she had seen during her forty years of being in the peace movement.

Be Careful: a misguided Listening to Learn effort could lead a community with real problems to believe that you are going to do something to help them, and you run the risk of getting people stirred up and then having no ability to help. Therefore, it is important that before you engage in Listening to Learn, you ask yourself the following questions:

1. Are there existing problems or conflicts that could be aggravated by getting people to talk about it?

2. Will we raise expectations for change that we can't help meet?

Chapter 24

Spontaneous Listening

Yes, every day of our lives we have opportunities to listen… to strangers, family, friends, antagonists…someone you are upset with, someone you want to grow closer to. Remember "One Mother's Story" in Chapter 3. We put that early in the book because listening in our daily lives is one of the greatest opportunities we have. That opportunity includes making mistakes and learning from them. As the author of this book, I can honestly say I've made most every mistake to be made, yet through it all I've grown and experienced wonderful changes in my life. Learning to listen is a life-long process that takes us ever deeper into greater understanding, compassion, and new possibilities.

Here is another story of spontaneous listening from Marion Pargamin. It bridges both the personal and the social aspects of listening.

Marion Pargamin's Story

Marion Pargamin is an Israeli woman living in Jerusalem. She was waiting for friends at Jerusalem's Jaffa Gate, when the following incident unfolded.

As I approach a bus stop, I notice two elderly men, an Arab and a Jew exchanging insults. Both are extremely angry with each other. I try to calm the Arab man, while some passing policemen try to calm the Jew. The bus arrives and the Jewish man gets aboard. The situation seems to settle down. But then a Jewish woman who did not get on the bus starts insulting the Arab man. He returns her insults. I try to calm them down, when a Palestinian woman bursts upon the scene and immediately assumes that the old Arab is under attack and rushes to rescue him. In an outrage, she begins to shout at the Jewish woman, who was finally beginning to calm down. The situation quickly heats up again.

It seems to me that the Palestinian woman is about to explode. I try to intervene, but she turns her fury on me, screaming out hatred, despair, and pain. The situation is an example of Palestine accusing Israel, and I represent Israel to her. The scenario is greater than the two of us, as it takes on significance far beyond this momentary conflict.

She shouts out her anger and sorrow about what is currently going on in the territories—the incursions of the Israeli military into Palestinian towns. She rants in particular about Jenin where some terrible fighting is currently taking place. She has family and friends there and she says that our soldiers are war criminals for what they are doing. She is convinced that we Israelis want to kill all Palestinians. Why do we hate them so much? she demands. Her people are not responsible for the Holocaust, so why should they be paying the price?

She confronts me about the refugees and describes their constant suffering—for which we are responsible. Pointing at the angry Jewish woman, she assures me that this Sephardi woman was treated with honor, as a human being, in an Arab country from where she comes. But look at how she behaves towards Palestinians now!

She rants on — shouting and spewing her hatred for Israel at me. I don't try to argue with her at all. I don't show any reaction to all these accusations. I just feel an overwhelming sense of compassion for her. I sense that I need to listen to her — simply listen as best I can. My patience is bolstered by an understanding that behind her overpowering hatred is deep suffering and pain—both of which have been aggravated by the current hostilities. Her agony must come out, before healing can take place.

To deal with the situation, I am prepared to listen to the worst of her accusations, distortions, and smears—without reacting. I am aware that what reinforces my strength at this moment is that I have absolutely no doubt that the suffering and pain of the Israeli people are equally real and legitimate. I don't let myself get tempted or drawn into feelings of guilt or anger. I feel deeply sorry for the tragedy and the pain on both sides.

To me, what is happening between us is not an issue of who is right and who is wrong. Thus I am able to feel very calm and peaceful deep inside. I sense that this is the only way to calm her fury. I let her vent and express her anger for a long time, without interrupting her. As she continues to shout at me, I begin to tell her that she has no need to yell, because I am listening to her with all my attention. I find myself caressing her arm. She lets me touch her, as she slowly lowers her voice, but continues to let her despair pour out.

She says to me, "Do you understand why some of us come to Israel and commit suicide among you? You are killing us anyway, so why not kill you in return?" Out of desperation, she even mentions the possibility of coming to Israel and blowing herself up. I tell her softly that I don't want her to die. Nobody should be driven to this kind of horrible decision. We all are suffering, on both sides. She continues on and on, claiming that the Zionists want to get rid of the Palestinians. I tell her, "You see, I am a Zionist and I don't want to get rid of you. I wish we could live together as good neighbors". She begins to listen to me!

She tells me about the Israeli demonstration that took place the week before, near Ramallah. She complains about the Jewish organizations who took part in it. Then she asks me to donate some money to buy phone cards for Palestinians who need them. I give her some money. By this time, the conversation between us is becoming quite normal. She has calmed down a lot and is not shouting any more.

She is almost relaxed, when I notice my friends approaching us. They are walking in a line—one hundred of them, one after the other, walking in silence—slowly, quietly, aware of each step. They

167

are creating an atmosphere of peace and safety around them.
Their presence radiates calm and warmth. I point them out to her
and explain that this is the reason I came here: to participate in a
peace walk, which Palestinians and Israelis are doing together. I
tell her about the walk and its message of coexistence and peace—
peace at every step, here and now.

I suggest that she might accompany me. She hesitates, but then
rejects my offer. As the group reaches us, several people I know
shake my hand warmly as they go by. I notice that my new
Palestinian friend is very moved by the walk and the atmosphere it
radiates. She seems to become calmer and more peaceful. She is
nothing like the furious woman I met only several minutes before.

The end of the line passes. I will join it. Again I invite her and
again she declines. I tell her that I understand and respect her
decision. Before I go I tell her, "I am sure that someday we will
succeed in building peace between us." She smiles and replies,
"Me too."

Then, to my total surprise, she approaches me and kisses me on my
cheeks! She walks alongside the line for a while. She tells me that
she likes this walk—that it makes her feel good. She says it brings
her relief and that her mood is much better now. I am deeply
moved. I feel overwhelmed by this encounter, especially by its
unexpected ending. Peace was there, just around the corner, and I
did not miss it! I was aware that an intense moment of true
reconciliation had taken place. So many things had contributed to
it: an incredible timing that brought me to this place at this time,
and that also brought her—with enough time to pour out her
anger, to receive the needed listening and compassion, and to calm
down, so that then she could be receptive to the subtle quiet energy
of the walk.

My friends' walk—emanating intense healing and bringing the
tangible presence of peace and goodwill of a dedicated group—
appeared just in time to complete the scene, adding a broader
perspective to a personal encounter. The thick walls of this
Palestinian woman's hatred were shattered—allowing her to

168

express what was deep in her heart. Kissing me was a miracle! Within a short period of time, laden with emotions, her energy of hatred and death underwent an incredible transformation. A seed of peace was sown in her heart. We must plant many more such seeds, and water them thoroughly.

Chapter 25

You Can Do It

This is where it all starts. You and I and every individual will have unlimited opportunities to practice deep listening with friends, family, neighbors, strangers—in discussing personal, interpersonal, social, political, religious, or any other issues. Here, we believe you will find, as we have, that listening can be a life-changing experience. Beyond encouraging positive communication, listening also brings us face to face with our own personal problems and limitations. These are the ingredients that challenge us to become more healthy and compassionate human beings. Deep listening reveals limitations, and it provides us with a means of going beyond those limitations.

The act of listening is no easier and no harder than the act of love—because in the end they are one in the same. What an adventure it is to grow into the challenge of both. As the authors of this book, you might think we are great listeners, but what you also need to know is that we have messed up throughout our lives and we continue to fall short at times. But that's where the adventure comes in because we also continue to learn and to grow. Indeed, we have been changed by those who have listened to and loved us—despite our struggles and limitations.

We are delighted to think that in reading this book you might take some new steps into the struggles, the blessings, and the adventure of deep listening.

www.ingramcontent.com/pod-product-compliance
Lightning Source LLC
Chambersburg PA
CBHW022231290526
45785CB00014B/717